Hugo's Simplified System

Portuguese in Three Months

Hugo's Language Books Limited

This enlarged edition
© 1985 Hugo's Language Books Ltd
All rights reserved
ISBN 0 85285 076 X

7th impression 1990

Written in 1983 by

Maria Fernanda S. Allen M.A., F.I.L.

Lecturer in Portuguese at the Polytechnic of Central London
(Post-Graduate Dept. and other courses) and Morley College;
Course Adviser on PGCE (post-graduate course for teachers);
Examiner for the Institute of Linguists.

Set in 9/11pt Linotron 202 Times by
Phoenix Photosetting
Printed and bound in Great Britain by
Courier International Ltd, Tiptree, Essex

Preface

This new edition of 'Portuguese in Three Months' has been written for us by Maria Allen, whose experience in teaching her native tongue ranges from beginners to post-graduate level. She has drawn on this expertise to produce a simple yet complete course for students aiming to acquire a good working knowledge of the language in a short time, and who will probably be studying alone at home.

The book begins with an explanation of Portuguese pronunciation, as far as this is possible without going too deeply into all the nuances and varying sounds involved. If you are working without a teacher, you should find that our system of 'imitated pronunciation' simplifies matters considerably. Using the book together with our cassette recordings (allowing you to hear the Portuguese text at the same time that you read it) is an ideal combination, giving another dimension to the course.

It has always been a principle of the Hugo method to teach only what is really essential. We assume that the student wants to learn Portuguese from a practical angle; the lessons contain those rules of grammar that will be of most use in this respect. Constructions are clearly explained, and the order in which everything is presented takes into consideration the need for rapid progress. Each lesson includes exercises and conversation drills; later in the course you will move on to the use of idiom and colloquialisms, so necessary for a thorough grasp of conversational Portuguese. Further help with reading and comprehension, in the form of extracts from modern authors and letter-writing styles, plus a selection of useful sentences and words arranged in phrasebook fashion and designed to widen your vocabulary, round off the course. An appendix lists verb formations and irregularities.

Ideally you should spend about an hour a day on your work (slightly less, maybe, if you do not use the cassette recordings), although there is no hard and fast rule on this. Do as much as you feel capable of doing; if you have no special aptitude for language-learning, there is no point in forcing yourself beyond your daily capacity to assimilate new material. It is much better to learn a little at a time, and to learn that thoroughly.

In studying the lessons, first read each rule or numbered section carefully and re-read it to ensure that you have fully understood the grammar, then translate the following exercise(s) by writing down the answers. Check these by referring to the key at the back of the book; if you have made too many mistakes, go back over the instruction before attempting the same questions again. The conversational exercises should be read aloud and their constructions carefully noted. If you have the cassette recordings, you should listen to these at the same time as you read the instruction and the examples. Listen also to the spoken Portuguese of each exercise, both before you complete the written work and again as you check the answers. After you have listened to the conversations and read them aloud, see how closely you can imitate the voices on the recording.

When you think you have completed a section satisfactorily (alternatively, just before your daily study period is over) go back over what you have recently done, to ensure that it is firmly committed to memory. Once you are through the first few lessons and have a good grasp of elementary grammar, dip into the idioms and reading passages, thereby increasing your vocabulary and your comprehension of both written and spoken Portuguese. When the course is completed, you should have a very good understanding of the language – more than sufficient for general holiday or business purposes, and enough to lead quickly into an examination syllabus if this is your eventual aim.

Contents

6

Pronunciation

In order to understand phonetics, and in particular our system of imitated pronunciation, it is essential to learn a few rules about syllables. These are groups of two or three letters which must include a vowel representing one sound.

A Portuguese word is automatically stressed on the last but one syllable (no accent mark is required) unless the word has an accent mark elsewhere or ends in an **l**, **r** or **z**. For example, **marmelada** has four syllables (ma me *la* da) and according to the rule it is stressed on the penultimate (*la*). As a result of this, the sound of the stressed *a* becomes open (ah) while the other a's remain mute (e^r).

Accent marks you will see in Portuguese are: the acute (´), the grave (`), the tilde (˜) and the circumflex (ˆ).

The Portuguese alphabet

A	B	C	D	E	F	G	H	I
(ah)	(bay)	(say)	(day)	(eh)	(eff)	(zhay*)	(e^r-gah**)	(ee)

J	L	M	N	O	P	Q	R	S
(*zhoh*-te^r)	(ell)	(emm)	(enn)	(oh)	(pay)	(kay)	(err)	(ess)

T	U	V	X	Z
(tay)	(oo)	(vay)	(sheesh)	(zay)

The letters K (*kah*-pe^r), W (*doo*-ble vay) and Y (ee-*gray*-goo) are not in use today, except when they refer to foreign names, chemistry symbols and so on.

* The G and J are pronounced like s in the English word 'measure'; this sound is represented by zh in our imitated pronunciation. When G has a hard sound (consult the imitated pronunciation guide that follows) it will be represented by g, as in 'girl'.

** Whenever you see a letter r in superscript (as in *zhoh*-te^r, *kah*-pe^r), usually after an e in the imitated syllables, remember that it is **not to be pronounced**. It is there in order to ensure that you give the correct sound; without this 'raised' r you might turn *kah*-pe^r into *kah*-pe – and make too much of the ending so that it became -pee, which would be quite wrong. Equally wrong would be -per.

The Imitated Pronunciation

Given the complex sound structure of Portuguese it is not always possible to transcribe its pronunciation in terms of English spelling. Nonetheless, the following notes should enable you to master with ease the most elusive as well as the most obvious Portuguese sounds. Of much greater help, naturally, would be the cassette recordings which Hugo's have produced; these allow you to hear the Portuguese words and phrases at the same time as you read them in the book. When studying this on your own, without a Portuguese teacher to talk to, then the complete Cassette Course makes everything much easier.

When reading the imitated pronunciation, avoid pauses between the syllables. Pronounce these as if they formed part of an English word, emphasising the one printed in italics – the stressed syllable. The Portuguese have an irrepressible tendency to link the sound of a terminal vowel with the beginning of the next word; this liaison results in **ele era** sounding like el-*leh*-r^e, or **nove horas** (*noh*'v^e and *oh*-re^{r}sh) becoming noh-*voh*-re^{r}sh.

Vowels

a

This is open (as in 'father') in a stressed syllable, before **l** or final **r**, and when it has an acute or grave accent. Otherwise it is mute, like the **u** in 'but'.

camada [ke^r-*mah*-de^r] layer	**animal** [e^r-nee-*mahl*] animal
falar [fe^r-*lahr*] to speak	**chá** [shah] tea

Becomes nasal when under a tilde mark (**ã**); the 'raised' or superscript ^{n} we use to indicate this sound should not be pronounced as a proper n, but more like the end of 'lung' without making much of the g.

  irmã [*eer*-ma^n] sister

When it is under a circumflex the **a** remains mute but its syllable, which is usually the third from the end, will be stressed instead of this falling on the usual last but one syllable.

  alfândega [al-*fa*^{n}-d^e-ge^r] Customs

e

Has an open sound (as in 'vet') in a stressed syllable, before **l** and under grave or acute accents. Unstressed, it is mute (as e in 'mute'). In Brazil, this mute sound is replaced by ee.

  metro [*meh*-troo] meter, underground (railway)
  café [ke^r-*feh*] coffee
  mel [mehl] honey
  secretária (s^e-kr^e-*tah*-ree-e^r) secretary

The 'close **e**', pronounced similarly to the e in 'seance', occurs in some stressed syllables, under a circumflex accent and before a final **r**.

  pelo [*pay*-loo] of the, by the

comer [koo-*mayr*] to eat
vê [vay] see
When an **e** is by itself or forms the first syllable on its own, it is
pronounced as the English e in 'see'.
   edifício [ee-dee-*fee*-sy'oo] edifice, building

i
This is always pronounced 'ee', but when unstressed it should be given a
shorter (close) sound.
   parti [pe^r-*tee*] I left

o
In a stressed position, or if it has an acute accent or comes before **l**, the
sound of **o** is open (similar to a in 'fall').
   avó [e^r-*voh*] grandmother
   sol [sohl] sun
   morte [*mohr*'t^e] death
It has a close sound similar to o in 'mole' in some stressed syllables, before
final **r**, and with the circumflex accent. This is the most used sound in
Brazil, with oo being heard at the end of a word.
   avô [e^r-*vo*] grandfather
   amor [e^r-*mor*] love
   folha [*fo*-l'ye^r] leaf
It has the sound of 'oo' in unstressed syllables and when it is on its own.
   tomar [too-*mahr*] to make
   gato [*gah*-too] cat
When it carries a tilde mark (õ) or precedes **n**, it has a nasal sound which
we imitate in the same way as explained under **ã**. See also the paragraph
dealing with nasal vowels and dipthongs.

u
This is always pronounced 'oo': **rua** [roo'e^r] street.

Oral dipthongs:

These are single vowel sounds resulting from the combination of two
vowels (or two vowels pronounced as one syllable). An example of a
dipthong in English is 'meat'. In Portuguese there are various
combinations, notably:

ai = i as in 'my'	**vai** [*vah*-ee] go, goes
ei = a as in 'tame'	**falei** [fe^r-*lay*-ee] I spoke
eu = ay'oo *	**meu** [may'oo] my
oi = oy'e *	**foi** [foy'e] went
ou = o	**falou** [fe^r-*lo*] he, you spoke

* As with the nasal dipthongs that follow, it is difficult to reproduce these
sounds on paper as they have no simple equivalents in English. Also note
that the ai/ei sounds can be imitated by ah'ee and ay'ee – sliding into the
second vowel, with a little more emphasis on the first.

Nasal vowels and dipthongs:

Whenever the vowels **a**, **e**, **i**, **o** and **u** precede **m** and **n**, they become nasal. If you have learned French, you should be familiar with the sound – for example, in *monter* or *environ*. It has already been pointed out that the 'raised' or superscript ^{n} we use to imitate this should not be pronounced fully; if you make the sound properly through your nose, there ought not to be much likelihood of error.

The same applies to the nasal dipthongs **ão**, **ãe**, **ãi** and **õe**, which we imitate as ah'oo^n, ah'e^n, ah'e^n and aw'i^n respectively.

encanto [e^n-*kahn*-too] charm	**untar** [oo^n-*tahr*] to grease
jardim [zher-*dee*^{n}] garden	**não** [nah'oo^n] no
ontem [*o*^{n}-te^n] yesterday	**limões** [lee-*maw*'i^{n}sh] lemons

Consonants

These are pronounced as in English, with the following exceptions:

c

This sounds like s in 'silver' when it comes before **e** or **i**; it is hard ('k') as in 'cat' when coming before **a**, **o** and **u**, unless it bears a cedilla (**ç**) which changes the sound to ss. The combination **ch** must be pronounced as an English sh.

cinema [see-*nay*-me^r] cinema	**começar** [koo-m^e-*sahr*] to begin
comer [koo-*mayr*] to eat	**chave** [*shah*-v^e] key

d

In Brazil, this is a harder sound almost as in English.

g

It sounds like the s in 'treasure', when coming before **e** or **i**. We imitate this by putting zh, but you must remember to pronounce it with your tongue further back from your teeth than in 'zoo'. Another similar sound is the French j, ge- or gi-.

    geral [zhe^r-*rahl*] general
    gigante [zhee-*ga*^{n}-t^e] giant

It is hard, as in 'get', before **a**, **o**, **u** and preceding a consonant.

    gordo [*gohr*-doo] fat

When in the combination **gu**, before **e** or **i**, the **u** is not pronounced.

    guerra [*gehr*-re^r] war
    guitarra [gee-*tahr*-re^r] guitar

h

This is never sounded.

j

Like the s in 'treasure'; it precedes **a**, **o**, **u**, but hardly ever **e**.

    jardim [zher-*dee*^{n}] garden
    joia [*zhoh*-ye^r] jewel

l

The final l is prolonged, but in Brazil it has a faint quality.
fácil [*fah*-seel] easy [*fah*-see'oo]

lh

Give this a liquid sound, like the lli in 'billiards'.
melhor [m^e-*l'yohr*] better
milho [*mee*-l'yoo] maize

nh

Pronounced as the ni in 'onion': minha [*mee*-n'ye^r] mine.

r

Has a soft sound, close to the Italian r in 'caro' or the second r in 'rare', when between vowels. It has a harder sound, like the well-rolled Scottish r or the first r in 'rare', when it is doubled or comes at the beginning of a word. At the end of a word or syllable it is prolonged still further. But in Brazil the final r is usually dropped.
barato (be^r-*rah*-too] cheap
carro [*kah*-rroo] car
amor [e^r-*mor*] love

s

As in 'salt' when beginning a word, doubled or after a consonant. Between vowels it is less sibilant, like s in 'rose' or z in 'zebra'. The final s of a word or syllable sounds like sh in 'sheep'. Brazilians sound a final s more as we do in English.
sonho [*so*-n'yoo] dream   lápis [*lah*-peesh] pencil
rosa [*roh*-ze^r] rose   cesto [*say*-shtoo] basket

t

Always as in 'tea'. In Brazil, like 'ch' – especially before e and i.

x

This has five sounds. It is like the English sh, when coming at the beginning of a word or between vowels. Also between vowels it can sound like s in 'some'. It has the sound of z when in the prefix ex plus a vowel, but is like ey'sh when ex is followed by a consonant. In words of foreign derivation it should be pronounced ks, as in English.
xadrez [she^r-*draysh*] chess   exército [ee-*zehr*-see-too] army
queixa [*kay*-she^r] complaint   explicar [ey'sh-plee-*kahr*] to explain
trouxe [tros^e] I bought   taxi [*tah*-ksee] taxi

z

Pronounce it as in 'zebra', except when it comes at the end of a word. A final z sounds like sh.
zanga [za^n-ge^r] anger
fazer [fe^r-*zayr*] to do, to make
luz [loosh] light

Introduction

Bom dia. [bo^n *dee*-e^r] Good morning.

Boa tarde. [*boh*-e^r *tahr*-d] Good afternoon.

Boa noite. [*boh*-e^r *noyt*] Good evening/good night.

Eu chamo-me Maria Fernanda Allen. [*ay*'oo *she^r*-moom . . .] My name is . . . (I am called . . .).

Como se chama o senhor? [*kom*-oo s^e *she^r*-me^r oo s^{e}n'*yor*] What is your name? (addressing a man).

Como se chama a senhora? [*kom*-oo s^e *she^r*-me^r e^r s^{e}n'*yor*-e^r] What is your name? (addressing a woman).

Como se chama você? [*kom*-oo se *she^r*-me^r *voh*-seh] What is your name? (casual 'you', either sex).

Sou a sua professora. [so e^r *soo*-e^r proof'*so*-re^r] I am your teacher.

Sou portuguesa. [so poor'too-*gay*-ze^r] I am Portuguese.

O senhor é inglês? [oo s^{e}n'*yor* eh eeng-*laysh*] Are you English? (addressing a man).

A senhora é inglesa? [e^r s^{e}n'*yor*-e^r eh eeng-*lay*-ze^r] Are you English? (addressing a woman).

Eu moro em Chelsea. [*ay*'oo *moh*-roo e^n . . .] I live in Chelsea.

Onde mora? [o^n'd *moh*-re^r] Where do you live?

Fala Português? [*fah*-le^r poor-too-*gaysh*] Do you speak Portuguese?

Não? [nah'oo^n) No?

Não faz mal. [nah-oo^n fahsh mahl] It does not matter.

Vamos agora aprender a falar português. [*ve^r*-moosh e^r-*goh*-re^r e^r-pre^n-*dair* e^r fe^r-*lahr* poor-too-*gaysh*] We are now going to learn (to speak) Portuguese.

Bracketed translations should be taken merely as a literal meaning of the idea expressed in the Portuguese idiom. Thus:

Idiomatic Portuguese	Idiomatic English
Precisa de ajuda?	Do you need any help? (*Literally* You need help?)
de dieta	on a diet (*Literally* of diet)

First lesson/primeira lição

1 Nouns

All Portuguese nouns are either masculine or feminine; there is no neuter 'it'. Nouns and adjectives ending in **o**, **im**, **om**, **um** are generally masculine while those ending in **a**, **ã**, **gem**, **dade**, **ice**, **ez**, **ção**, **são** are feminine. Nouns ending in **r**, **l**, **e** are not necessarily masculine (as is often wrongly stated), for they have an equal chance of being feminine. For example:

a flor (*f*) the flower, but **o amor** (*m*) love
a capital (*f*) the capital (of a country), but **o animal** (*m*) the animal
a noite (*f*) the evening, night, but **o perfume** (*m*) the perfume

More on the identification of the gender in section 21, page 47

The plural

The plural of nouns and adjectives is formed, in general, by adding **s** to those ending in a vowel, and **es** to those ending in a consonant. For other rules regarding the plural see section 22, page 49

2 The definite article

'The' agrees with the noun in gender and number, as seen in the examples given in section 1.

'The' = **o** [oo] *m sing*   **os** [oosh] *m pl*
        a [e^r] *f sing*   **as** [e^{r}sh] *f pl*

More on the definite article in section 49, page 107

Exercise 1

Please fill in the blanks with the appropriate article:
1 — **rapariga** [re^r-pe^r-*ree*-ge^r] (*in Brazil:* **moça** [*moh*-se^r]) the girl
2 — **rapaz** [re^r-*pahsh*] the boy
3 — **escritório** [ish-kree-*toh*-re'o] the office
4 — **casa** [*kah*-ze^r] the house, home
5 — **flores** [flo'rsh] the flowers

6 — **empregos** [e^n-*pray*-goosh] the jobs, employment
7 — **gatos** [*gah*-toosh] the cats
8 — **alunas** [e^r-*loo*-ne^{r}sh] the pupils

3 The indefinite article

'A', 'an' are translated in Portuguese as **um** before a masculine noun in the singular, and **uma** is the feminine equivalent. Unlike English, these articles have plural forms **uns** (*m*) **umas** (*f*), which are best translated as 'some' or not translated at all. For example:

um homem [oo^n *oh*-me^n] a man
uns homens [oo^{n}sh *oh*-me^{n}sh] men, some men
uma mulher [*oo*-me^r mool-*yair*] a woman
umas mulheres [*oo*-me^{r}sh mool-*yairsh*] women, some women

Exercise 2

Please fill in the blanks with the appropriate indefinite article:
1 — **viagem** [vee-*ah*-zhe^n] a trip
2 — **escritório** an office
3 — **avião** [e^r-vee-*ah*-oo^n] a plane
4 — **cidade** [see-*dah*-d^e] a city, town
5 — **bilhete** [beel-*yay*-t^e] a ticket (*m*)
6 — **homens** men
7 — **mulheres** women
8 — **viagens** [vee-*ah*-zhe^{n}sh] trips, voyages, travels
9 — **escritórios** offices
10 — **raparigas** girls

4 Present tense of verb 'ter' (to have)

Singular

eu tenho [*ay*'oo *te^{r}n*-yoo]	I have
tu tens [too te^n'sh]	you (*familiar*) have
você tem [*voh*-seh te^n]	you have
o senhor tem [oo s^{e}n-*yor* te^n]	you (*formal*) have
a senhora tem [e^r s^{e}n-*yor*-e^r te^n]	you (*formal*) have
ele tem [ell te^n]	he has
ela tem [*eh*-le^r te^n]	she has

Plural

nós temos [nosh *tay*-moosh]	we have
vocês têm [*voh*-sehs *tay*'ing]	you (*familiar pl*) have
os senhores têm [oosh s^{e}n'*yorsh*. . .]	you (*formal*) have (*m*)
as senhoras têm [e^{r}sh s^{e}n'*yor*-e^{r}sh. . .]	you (*formal*) have (*f*)
eles têm [ellsh *tay*'ing]	they have (*m*)
elas têm [*ehl*-e^{r}sh *tay*'ing]	they have (*f*)

Portuguese has several forms of the personal pronoun with which you will need to become acquainted. **Tu** is the familiar form. This is seldom used in Brazil. **Você** is neither familiar nor very formal and is the form most commonly used in Brazil. **O senhor** is used when addressing a man formally and **a senhora** is its feminine equivalent. **Vocês** is the plural equivalent of **tu** and **você**, and **os senhores** and **as senhoras** are formal forms.

4a Expressions with the verb 'ter' which in English use the verb 'to be'

ter fome [tair-fohm] to be hungry
ter sede [said] to be thirsty
ter frio [*free*'oo] to be cold
ter calor [ke^r-*lohr*] to be warm
ter sono [*soh*-noo] to be sleepy

ter razão [re^r-*zah*'oo^n] to be right
ter pressa [*preh*-se^r] to be in a hurry
ter vinte anos [*vee^n*-t' *ee^r*-noosh] to be twenty years old

ter saudades [se^r'oo-*dah*-d'sh] to feel longing, nostalgia for, to miss *e.g.* **Tenho saudades de Portugal.** [poor-too-*gahl*] I miss Portugal.

Que é que tem? [kee'*eh* k^e te^{n}g] What is the matter with you?

ter de or **ter que** expresses a strong necessity or obligation. For example:

Tenho que terminar este trabalho. [*te^{r}n*-yoo k^e terr-mee-*nahr* esht tre^r-*bahl*'yoo] I have to finish this work.
Você tem de partir imediatamente. [pe^r-*teer* em-d'*yah*-te^r-*me^{n}t*] You must leave immediately.

5 Negative of verbs

'Not' and 'don't' are translated by **não** [*nah*'oo^n], which is placed before the verb.

Eu não tenho dinheiro. [deen-*yay*'e-roo] I have no money.

Não also means 'no'.

5a Interrogative form

Just give an enquiring intonation to the statement; *e.g.* **Tem troco?** Have you any change?
Sometimes you may put the subject after the verb; *e.g.* **Que disse você?** What did you say?

6 The verb 'haver' (to have)

'There is'/'there are'. Used mainly in the third person singular, with the meaning of 'there is', 'there are', 'ago' and 'for' (relating to time), it corresponds to the French *il y a*, the Spanish *hay*, the Italian *c'è:*

Há muita gente aqui. [ah m*wee*^{n}-te^r ge^n-t' e^r-*kee*] There are a lot of people here.
Há quanto tempo está em Lisboa? [ah *kwa*^{n}-too *te*^{n}-poo ish-*tah* e^n leesh-*bo*'e^r] (For) how long have you been in Lisbon?
O avião partiu há cinco minutos. [oo e^r-ve-*ah*'oo^n pe^r-t'*yoo* ah *see*^{n}-koo mee-*noo*-toosh] The plane left five minutes ago.

Haver de [e^r-*vair*' d] fully conjugated in the present tense, plus the infinitive of another verb, expresses an action in the future. It implies a strong intention, equivalent to 'I will':

Hei-de ir ao Brasil. I will go to Brazil.

Present tense

Singular

eu hei-de [*ay*'oo aid^e]	I will . . .
tu hás-de [too *ahsh*'d^e]	you will . . . (*familiar*)
você há-de [*voh*-seh ah-d^e]	you will . . . (*informal*)
ele há-de [el ah-d^e]	he will . . .
ela há-de [*eh*-le^r ah'd^e]	she will . . .

Plural

nós havemos de [nosh e^r-*vay*-moosh'd^e]	we will . . .
vocês hão-de [*voh*-sehs *ah*'oo^{n}d^e]	you will . . . (*familiar*)
eles hão-de [ellsh *ah*'oo^n-d^e]	they will . . . (*m*)
elas hão-de [*ehl*-e^{r}sh *ah*'oo^n-d^e]	they will . . . (*f*)

7 Subject pronouns

eu 'I', **tu** 'you', **nós** 'we' are frequently omitted except for the purpose of emphasis or because the verb ending indicates who is performing the action.

tu 'you' (*familiar*) is used among friends, relatives, and in addressing children. It is seldom used in Brazil.

você 'you' (not familiar but *informal*) is used mainly between persons of the same age group or from employer to employee, teacher to student etc. It is widely used in Brazil.
Vocês 'you', plural is used both as the familiar and informal form.

O senhor, a senhora, os senhores, as senhoras are the most polite forms of rendering 'you'. when addressing a man, woman, men, women. When addressing a mixed group of people, the masculine form is used.
Você and **o senhor/a senhora** take the third person singular, the same as **ele** 'he' and **ela** 'she'. **Vocês, as senhoras/os senhores** take the third person plural, the same as **eles, elas** 'they'.

The word for 'you' may be omitted completely once the form of address has been established in a particular situation. For example:

Falas Português? Do you (*familiar*) speak Portuguese?
Fala Português? Do you (*informal* or *formal*) speak Portuguese?

There is another plural 'you', **vós**, but we shall ignore it in this course because it is no longer used, and is found only in classical texts, prayers etc.

Exercise 3

Translate the following:
1 Tenho.
2 Você tem?
3 Não temos.
4 Vocês têm.
5 Ela tem?
6 Os senhores não têm.

7 I have no money.
8 Have you (*f sing formal*) a ticket?
9 They have good jobs.
10 Have you (*pl informal*) a house?
11 You (*sing familiar*) have an office.
12 We are hungry.
13 There is a table.
14 How long have you (*formal*) been speaking English?

See exercises 1 and 2 for vocabulary. Note additionally:
mesa [*may*-se^r] table

CONVERSATIONAL SENTENCES

1
A Bom dia. O senhor tem cigarros ingleses com filtro?
B Agora não tenho, desculpe. Mas aquela loja à esquina tem cigarros ingleses, com certeza.
A Obrigado.

2
A Você tem tempo para um café?
B Sim, tenho, com muito prazer.
A Então vamos aqui ao lado. Têm um café muito bom e há pouca gente.

3
A Os seus amigos ainda têm o andar em Lisboa?
B Agora não, mas têm uma linda casa no Algarve, com um grande jardim e piscina.
A Que sorte! Quem me dera ter uma casa assim!
B Eu também.

New words and their imitated pronunciation:
1
cigarros ingleses [see-*gah*-rroosh een-*glay*-shesh] English cigarettes
com [ko^n] with
agora não [e^r-*goh*-re^r nah-oo^n] not at the moment
desculpe [d'sh-*kool*-p^e] I'm sorry
mas [me^{r}sh] but
aquela [e^r-*kay*-le^r] that (*f sing*)
loja [*loh*-zhe^r] shop
esquina [esh-*kee*-ne^r] corner
com certeza [ko^n s^{e}r-*tay*-ze^r] definitely, certainly, for sure

2
tempo para [te^n-poo per'e^r] time for
muito prazer [moo'i^n-too pre^r-*zayr*] great pleasure
então [e^n'*tah*'oon] then, in that case
vamos aqui ao lado [ve^r-moosh e^r-*kee* ah'oo *lah*-doo] let's go next door
pouca gente [*poh*-ke^r zhe^n-t^e] not many people, few people

3
Os seus amigos ainda têm o andar em Lisboa? [osh *say*'osh e^r-*mee*-gosh e^r-*een*-de^r *tay*'ing oo an-*dahr* e^n leesh-*boh*-e^r] Do your friends still have the flat in Lisbon?
linda [lee^n-de^r] beautiful
grande [$grah^n$-de] big, large
jardim [zhe^r-dee^n] garden
piscina [peesh-*see*-ne^r] swimming pool
que sorte! [k^e *sohr*-t^e] what luck!, how fortunate!
quem me dera [ke^n m' *deh*-re^r] how I wish . . .
assim [e^r-ssi^n] like that
eu também [*ay*'oo tah^n-*ben*] me too, so would I

Second lesson/segunda lição

8 'Ser' and 'estar'

The irregular verbs ser [sair] and estar [ish-*tahr*] both mean 'to be', but they have different rôles. In general, ser denotes an inherent or permanent quality of 'being', and a profession or calling, even if *temporary*. It is wrong to say the verb ser is permanent, and to leave the student to sort out the confusion which will come later. There is nothing permanent about sou um aluno 'I am a student'; nor indeed about sou um turista 'I am a tourist'. The same can be said for sou solteiro 'I am single/a bachelor'. In short, ser is *what* you are, or *who* you are. The following examples will clarify the point:

Sou portuguesa. I (*f*) am Portuguese.
Lisboa é linda. Lisbon is beautiful.
Ele é casado. He is married.
Nós somos amigos. We are friends.

8a 'Ser' plus the preposition 'de'

Ser plus the preposition de denotes possession, origin. Where there is a possessive adjective or pronoun, de is omitted:

Eles são de Londres. They are from London.
Esta chave é do senhor Gomes. This key belongs to Mr Gomes.
Esta casa é minha. This house is mine.

Ser is also used for the passive voice, impersonal phrases, telling the time, and permanent location (a well-known place). For example:

Este trabalho é sempre feito por mim. This work is always done by me.
É importante. It is important.
É uma hora da tarde. It is 1.00 pm.
Onde é o castelo de Windsor? Where is Windsor Castle?

8b 'Estar'

Estar is used when speaking of a temporary state or condition, action, and place.

Eles estão em Londres. They are in London. When comparing this example to the preceding, which uses **ser**, notice the prepositions are different: birthplace uses **de** and location uses **em**; this is another clue – if you see **em** you know that **estar** must be used.

Temporary state or condition
Ela está feia. She is looking ugly.
(*But:* **Ela é feia.** She is ugly.)
Nós estamos cansados. We are tired.

Estar plus the preposition **a** followed by the infinitive is used to express the present continuous tense. For example:

Eu estou a trabalhar. I am working.
(In Brazil, the present participle is used instead of the infinitive. Thus: **Eu estou trabalhando.**)

Estar com expresses the same meaning as **ter** in expressions such as:

Estou com fome (= Tenho fome) I am hungry.
Estou com sono (= Tenho sono) I am sleepy.
See also section 4a, page 15

8c Present tenses

	ser	estar
eu (I)	**sou** [so]	**estou** [ish-*to*]
tu (you *familiar*)	**és** [ehsh]	**estás** [ish-*tahsh*]
você (you *informal*)	**é** [eh]	**está** [ish-*tah*]
ele, ela (he, she)	**é**	**está**
nós (we)	**somos** [*so*-moosh]	**estamos** [ish-*te^r*-moosh]
vocês (you (*pl informal*)	**são** [*sah*-oo^n]	**estão** [ish-*tah*-oo^n]
os senhores (you *formal m pl*)	**são**	**estão**
as senhoras (you *formal f pl*)	**são**	**estão**
eles, elas (they *m f*)	**são**	**estão**

Please refer to the subject pronouns given in section 7, page 17.

Sentences with the verbs **ser** *and* **estar**:

Ela é linda. She is beautiful.
Ela está linda. She is looking beautiful.
O homem é velho. The man is old.
O homem está velho. The man is getting old.
Elas são aborrecidas. They (*f pl*) are boring.
Elas estão aborrecidas. They are bored.

Eu sou enganada por todos. I (*f sing*) am misled (cheated, taken for a ride) by everyone.
Eu estou enganada. I am mistaken.

Key to pronunciation:

linda [*lee*ⁿ-de^r); **velho** [*vehl*-yoo]; **aborrecidas** [e^r-boor-r^e-*seed*-e^{r}sh]; **enganada** [eⁿ-ge^r-*nah*-de^r]; **por todos** [poor *to*-doosh].

Exercise 4 (on ser)

1 I (*f*) am English.
2 Are you the manager of this hotel?
3 He is boring.
4 She is a secretary.
5 This is very important.
6 We (*f*) are friends.
7 They (*m*) are old.
8 Are these the suitcases? (*meaning* your suitcases)
9 Estas malas não são minhas.
10 Isto é impossível.
11 Eu não sou secretária, sou professora.
12 Nós somos amigas.
13 Vocês são casados?

Vocabulary and key to pronunciation:

inglesa [eeⁿ-*glay*-ze^r] English (*f*)
gerente [j^e-*re*ⁿ-t^e] manager
deste [daysh-t^e] of this
hotel [o-*tel*] hotel
secretária [s^e-kr^e-*tah*-ree-e^r] secretary
isto [*eesh*-too] this
importante [eeⁿ-poor'*ta*ⁿ-t^e] important
estas [*ehsh*-te^{r}sh] these
malas [*mah*-le^{r}sh] suitcases
minhas [*meen*-ye^{r}sh] mine (*f*)
impossível [eeⁿ-poss-*ee*-vel] impossible
casados [ke^r-*zah*-doosh] married

Exercise 5 (on estar)

1 I am in London.
2 Are you (*f familiar*) tired?
3 She is not at home.
4 We are working every day.
5 They (*m*) are mistaken.
6 The train is late.

7 Estou a comer.
8 Você está hoje em casa?
9 Nós não estamos enganados.
10 O senhor está com fome.
11 Elas estão lindas.
12 As raparigas estão prontas.

Vocabulary and key to pronunciation:

Londres [lo^n-dr^{e}sh] London
cansadas [ka^n-*sah*-de^{r}sh] tired (*f pl*)
em casa [e^n-*kah*-se^r] at home
trabalhar [tre^r-be^{r}l-*yahr*] to work
todos os dias [*to*-doosh oosh *dee*-e^{r}sh] every day
o comboio [oo ko^n-*boh*'e-oo] the train (*In Brazil*, 'train' is **trem**.)
atrasado [e^r-tre^r-*zah*-doo] late
comer [koo-*mayr*] to eat
hoje [o-zh^e] today
fome [*foh*-m^e] hunger
prontas [*pro^n*-te^{r}sh] ready (*f pl*)

9 Adjectives

Adjectives agree in gender and number with the noun they qualify and they usually follow it. For example: **a lingua portuguesa** the Portuguese language. As with nouns, the masculine ending of an adjective **o** changes to **a**, if the noun is feminine. If it ends in **s, z, r**, you add **a**. Adjectives ending in other consonants or **e** do not change in the feminine. In the plural adjectives behave like nouns. For additional rules see sections 21 and 22.

When the adjective precedes the noun, its meaning may be modified. For example:

um homem pobre a poor man (meaning he has no money)
um pobre homem a poor man (a man to be pitied on account of some misfortune)

Grande before a noun usually means 'great'. When it follows a noun, it means 'big' or 'large'. For example:

um grande homem a great man (meaning distinguished)
um homem grande a big man (referring to his physique)

But there are a number of other adjectives which preferably are placed before the noun:

bom/boa good
belo/bela beautiful
mau/má bad

longo/longa long
breve soon, short
muito/muita* much
muitos/muitas many

Note also that the ordinal numbers usually precede the noun, as in English:
no terceiro dia on the third day.

The adjectives in Portuguese often serve as past participles which also agree in number and gender with the subject: **elas estão cansadas** they are tired.

* **Muito** as an adverb, meaning 'very much' or 'very', is invariable.

10 Main prepositions

de [d^e] of, from
em [e^n] in, on, at
a [e^r] at, to
por [poohr] for, by, through
para [pe^r re^r] for, to, in order to. (*See section 48, page 105.*)

Some of these prepositions combine with the articles as follows:
de plus **o, a, os, as** becomes **do, da, dos, das** of the.

de plus the indefinite article becomes **dum, duma, duns, dumas** of a, of some (although in this case they could also be separated).

em plus the above becomes: **no, na, nos, nas** in the, on the, at the.

num, numa, nuns, numas in a, in some, etc (sometimes separated).

a plus the definite article becomes: **ao, à, aos, às** to the, at the. (It does not combine with the indefinite article.)

Por plus the definite article becomes: **pelo, pela, pelos, pelas** by the, etc. It does not combine with any other part of speech.

Para does not combine with any part of speech.

The first three prepositions also join demonstrative adjectives and also 3rd persons of object pronouns, i.e. **dele** of him, his, **dela** of her, hers, etc.

Possessive case

The preposition **de** and its combined forms indicate the possessive case in Portuguese. For example:

Mary's house **A casa da Maria**.

Please refer to section 46, page 104.

Exercise 6

Translate the following:
1 The book is on the table.
2 The woman is at the door.
3 She is going through the park.
4 Uncle Tom's office.
5 I am on the (at the) telephone.
6 Vamos ao mercado.
7 Vou para casa.
8 Ela está na casa de banho.
9 Numa situação como esta.
10 Ele entrou pela janela.
11 Falo do acidente.
12 Ele deu o dinheiro ao rapaz.

Vocabulary and key to pronunciation:
o livro [*lee*-vroo] the book
mesa [*may*-se^r] table
porta [*pohr*-te^r] door
ela vai [*eh*-le^r *vah*-ee] she is going
o parque [park] park
tio Tomás [*tee*-oo too-*mahsh*] uncle Tom
o telefone [oo t^e-*l^e*-foh-n^e] the telephone
mercado [m^{e}r-*kah*-doo] market
vou [voh] I am going
casa [*kah*-ze^r] home, house
casa de banho [*be^{r}n*'yoo] bathroom (*In Brazil*: 'bathroom' is **banheiro**.)
como esta [*koh*-moo *ehsh*-te^r] like this (one)
situação [see-too-e^r-*sa*'oo^n] situation
ele entrou [el e^n-*troh*] he came in
janela [zhe^r-*neh*-le^r] window
falo do . . . [*fah*-loo doo] I speak about the . . .
acidente [e^r-see-*de^n*-t^e] accident
ele deu [el day'oo] he gave

CONVERSATION

Um encontro/a meeting

Sr Smith	Olá Dona Linda. Como está?
Sra Pereira	Estou bem, obrigada. E você?
Sr Smith	Bem, obrigado.
Sra Pereira	Então por aqui?
Sr Smith	Sim, **estou aqui há dois dias**, em negócios.

26

Sra Pereira	E **quanto tempo vai ficar** em Lisboa?
Sr Smith	**Vou ficar uma semana**, pelo menos. Estou na casa dos meus amigos Bosomworth. Você lembra-se deles?
Sra Pereira	Sim, muito bem, por causa do nome. Creio que o nome deles quer dizer em Português, 'peito de valor'. Que cómico!
Sr Smith	Não é mais cómico que o seu, que quer dizer em Inglês 'beautiful peartree'.
Sra Pereira	Bem, é uma questão de opinião. Ah aqui vem a minha amiga Angélica. Angélica, apresento-lhe o Sr. Tomás Smith . . . Doutora Angélica dos Santos da Purificação.
Sr Smith	Muito prazer, minha senhora.
Dra Santos da P.	Igualmente.
Sr Smith	Desculpe, por favor repita o seu nome, e devagar. Não compreendi bem.
Dra Santos da P.	Angélica dos Santos da Purificação.
Sr Smith	Que pureza, senhora doutora!
Sra Pereira	Bem, desculpe Tomás, mas **temos que** nos ir embora. Estamos com muita pressa. Telefone-me. Adeus.
Sr Smith	Adeus Dona Linda e Doutora Angélica. Até breve.

Key to the conversation:

Mr Smith	Hello (Mrs) Linda. How are you?
Mrs Pereira	I am very well, thank you. And you?
Mr Smith	Well, thank you. (*Notice a man says* obrigado *and a woman says* obrigada)
Mrs Pereira	Fancy meeting you here. (*literally* Are you here then?)
Mr Smith	Yes, **I have been here two days**, on business.
Mrs Pereira	And **how long are you going to stay** (are you staying) in Lisbon?
Mr Smith	**I am going to stay** (am staying) **for one week**, at least. I am at my friends the Bosomworths' house. Do you remember them?
Mrs Pereira	Yes, very well, because of their name. I believe their name (*literally* the name of them) means in Portuguese, 'peito de valor'. How funny!
Mr Smith	No more than yours which means in English, 'beautiful peartree'.
Mrs Pereira	Well, it is a matter of opinion. Ah, here comes my friend Angela. Angela, let me introduce (to you) Mr Thomas Smith . . . Dr Angela dos Santos da Purificação.
Mr Smith	Pleased to meet you.
Santos da P.	Likewise. (*literally* Equally.)

Mr Smith	I am sorry, please repeat your name, and slowly. I didn't understand (it) well.
Santos da P.	Angela of the Saints of the Purification.
Mr Smith	What purity, dear doctor!
Mrs Pereira	Well, I am sorry but **we** (shall have to) **have to go**. We are in a hurry. Ring me up. Good-bye.
Mr Smith	Good-bye Linda and Dr Angela. See you soon.

The Portuguese present tense translates the:

English present simple tense (e.g. I stay)
English present continuous tense (e.g. I am staying)
English future with intention tense (e.g. I am *going to* stay)
English future tense (e.g. we shall have to go)

See also section 32, page 73 *Other ways of expressing the future*.

In certain expressions, the English perfect tense is also expressed in the Portuguese present, for example:

Estou aqui há dois dias. I have been here for two days.
However, this latter example owes its meaning more to the idiomatic use of **há** (see explanation on the uses of 'há' in section 6, page 16.)

11 Forms of address

Sr stands for **Senhor** 'Mr' and of course don't forget it also means 'you' when addressing a man formally. **Sra** is the written abbreviation for **Senhora** 'Mrs' and also 'you'. When addressing a married woman, you use her Christian name preceded by Senhora Dona (Sra D). In Brazil, just 'Dona' is sufficient. If you do not know her Christian name, then Senhora (Sra) plus her surname is the usual form of address. Use the abbreviated form when writing (on envelopes etc.). Domestic helpers and tradespeople are normally addressed as Senhora (Sra) plus their Christian name. In Brazil, **Seu** is a common way of addressing male tradespeople. For example: 'Seu José'. Unmarried women (up to a certain age) may be addressed as **Menina** or just by their first name. In some cases 'Menina' is used when addressing shopkeepers, switchboard girls, and so on. In Brazil, **Senhorita** would be used instead.

The student is advised to listen well to the Portuguese people addressing each other in private and public places, before attempting to venture through the maze of Portuguese forms of address, their various degrees of formality and class distinction which are still in existence.

When addressing a doctor (medicine, law, PhD), **Senhor doutor** (Sr Dr) is used. For example: **Como está o Senhor doutor?** How are you, doctor? (**Senhora doutora** for a woman doctor). When addressing an engineer (university level) use **Senhor engenheiro** (Sr Eng). An architect (university level) is **Senhor arquitecto** (Sr Arq).

Please repeat the following expressions from the previous conversation:
em negócios [e^n n^e-*goh*-see-oosh] on business
pelo menos [*pay*-loo *may*-noosh] at least
lembra-se de . . ? [*le^n*-bre^{r}s^e d^e] do you remember?
creio que [*kray*-o k^e] I believe
quer dizer [kehr dee-*zayr*] it means
apresento-lhe [e^r-pr^e*ze^n*-too-l'y^e] I introduce to you
muito prazer [*mwee^n*-too pre^r-*zayr*](It's a) great pleasure, how do you do?
igualmente (ee-*gwahl*-me^n-t^e) likewise (This is a useful little word that is used when reciprocating a wish or returning a compliment, and avoids repeating 'Muito prazer', 'Boa sorte' Good luck, 'Feliz Natal' Happy Christmas, etc.)

Third lesson/terceira lição

12 Regular verbs

There are three conjugations, which end in **-ar**, **-er**, **-ir**. The part of the verb which precedes these terminations is called the *stem*. To conjugate any verb belonging to its respective conjugation all you have to do is to preserve the stem and add the appropriate endings as shown below. The endings are given in bold type. These must be learned because they indicate who is performing the action, since the personal pronoun is often omitted.

Present tense

	falar (to speak)	**comer** (to eat)	**abrir** (to open)
eu (I)	fal**o**	com**o**	abr**o**
tu (you *familiar*)	fal**as**	com**es**	abr**es**
você (you *informal*)	fal**a**	com**e**	abr**e**
ele, ela (he, she)	fal**a**	com**e**	abr**e**
nós (we)	fal**amos**	com**emos**	abr**imos**
vocês (you *pl informal*)	fal**am**	com**em**	abr**em**
eles, elas (they *m, f*)	fal**am**	com**em**	abr**em**

Key to pronunciation:

First conjugation: *fah*-loo, *fah*-le^{r}sh, *fah*-le^r, fe^r-*le^r*-moosh, *fah*-law^n
Second conjugation: *ko*-moo, *koh*-m^{e}sh, *koh*-m^e, koo-*meh*-moosh, *koh*-me^n
Third conjugation: *ah*-broo, *ah*-br^{e}sh, *ah*-br^e, e^r-*bree*-moosh, *ah*-bre^n

Exercise 7 (*see vocabulary below*)

1 Procuramos uma casa.
2 Eles não falam Português muito bem, mas compreendem tudo.
3 Ela nunca aceita o meu convite.
4 Que toma o senhor?
5 Ele abre a janela.
6 Estudo todos os dias.
7 Vocês não comem muito.
8 Parto às nove horas.

Vocabulary and key to pronunciation:

procurar [proo-koo-*rahr*] to look for
muito bem [moo'*i*^{n}-too be^n] very well
compreender [ko^n-pre-e^n-*dayr*] to understand
perceber [pe^r-se^r-*bayr*] to understand
tudo [*too*-doo] everything
nunca [*noo*^{n}-ke^r] never
aceitar [e^r-sa-*tahr*] to accept
meu [*may*-oo] my (*also* mine)
convite [ko^n-*vee*-t^e] invitation
que [k^e] what
tomar [too-*mahr*] to take, to have food or drink
estudar [ish-too-*dahr*] to study
todos os dias [*to*-doosh oosh *dee*-e^{r}sh] every day
partir [pe^r-*tee*^{r}] to leave, to depart
às nove horas [ahsh *noh*-v^e *oh*-re^{r}sh] at nine o'clock

Exercise 8

Translate into Portuguese:
1 My brother is looking for a job in Mozambique.
2 He is learning Portuguese.
3 Do you need help?
4 I accept your invitation with pleasure.
5 They drink and smoke too much.
6 The train leaves on schedule.
7 He is selling his car.
8 Today I am not buying anything.
9 My sister does not eat at one o'clock.
10 She is on a diet.

Vocabulary and key to pronunciation:

meu irmão [*may*-oo eer-*mah*'oo^n] my brother
Moçambique [moo-sa^n-*bee*-k^e] Mozambique
aprender [e^r-pre^n-*dayr*] to learn
precisar de [pr^e-see-*zahr* d^e] to need
ajuda [e^r-*joo*-de^r] help
seu [*say*-oo] your (*formal*)
beber [b^e-*bayr*] to drink
fumar [foo-*mahr*] to smoke
demasiado [d^e-me^r-zee-*ah*-doo] too much
partir [per-*teer*] to leave
à tabela [ah te^r-*bay*-le^r] on time, on schedule (*In Brazil:* **no horário certo**)
vender [ve^n-*dayr*] to sell
carro [*kahr*-roo] car
comprar [ko^n-*prahr*] to buy

nada [*nah*-de^{r}] nothing
minha irmã [*mee*-n'ye^{r} eer-*ma*^{n}] my sister
almoço [al-*mo*-soo] lunch
de dieta [d^{e} dee-*ay*-te^{r}] on a diet

13 Interrogative and relative pronouns

como? [*ko*-moo] how
Como está? How are you? (*sing.*)
Como se chama? What is your name? (*literally* How are you called?)
Como se diz 'table' em português? How do you say 'table' in Portuguese?
(Although not relevant to this paragraph note that 'como' also means 'as',
'like', and of course 'I eat'.)

quando? [*kwa*^{n}-doo] when?
Quando vai ao Brasil? When are you going to Brazil?

onde? [o^{n}-d^{e}] where?
Onde moram os senhores? Where do you (*pl formal*) live?

quem? [ke^{n}] who?
Quem foi que fêz isto? Who was it that did this?

porque? [poor'-*k*^{e}] why? (also 'because')
Porque vai a Lisboa? Why are you (*sing. formal*) going to Lisbon?

que [k^{e}], **o que** [oo k^{e}] what, that, which
Que diz você? What do you say? What are you saying?
Que deseja? What do you want? What would you like?
Que rua? Which street?

quanto? [*kwa*^{n}-too] (*m*) **quanta?** [*kwa*^{n}-te^{r}] (*f*) how much
Quanto custa? How much does it cost?

quantos [*kwa*^{n}-toosh] (*m*) **quantas** [*kwa*^{n}-te^{r}sh] (*f*) How many?
Quantos quartos deseja? How many bedrooms do you want?
Quantas libras deseja trocar? How many pounds do you want to change?

qual [kwal], **quais** [*kwa*'eesh] (*pl*) which (*see* relative pronouns)
Qual é o melhor hotel aqui? Which is the best hotel here?
Quais são as calças que prefere? Which are the trousers that you (*formal*)
prefer?

O quê? What? when used on its own as an exclamation.

Porquê? [poor-*kay*] Why? when used on its own or followed by 'que'.
Porquê que fez isso? Why did you do it? (*literally* Why is it that you did it?)
quem [ke^n] as a relative pronoun is used after prepositions, meaning 'whom', 'whose'. For example:

De quem é esta caneta? Whose pen is this?
Para quem é esta carta? Who is this letter for? (*literally* For whom is this letter?)
Não sei a quem devo pagar. I do not know (to) whom I must pay.

When not preceded by prepositions, 'who' and 'whom' are translated by **que**. **Que** as a relative pronoun 'who', 'that', 'which' is used more often in Portuguese than in English. For example:

Este é o livro que ele me deu. This is the book which he has given me.
As flores que você me comprou, são muito bonitas. The flowers which you have bought me are very pretty.
Foi a sua amiga que me informou. It was your friend who informed me.

O que 'what' as a relative pronoun:
Não compreendo o que você diz. I do not understand what you are saying.

The relative pronouns **cujo, cuja, cujos cujas** [*koo*-zhoo, *koo*-zhe^r, *koo*-zhoosh, *koo*-zhe^{r}sh] 'of which', 'whose' agree in gender and number with the noun to which they refer. For example:

A minha secretária, cuja mãe vive na América do Norte, vai-se embora. My secretary, whose mother lives in North America, is going away.
A sua carta, cujo conteúdo me surpreendeu . . . Your letter, the contents of which surprised me . . .

o qual, a qual, os quais, as quais as relative pronouns are often used instead of **que** for better clarification when there is more than one antecedent. For example:

A irmã do meu amigo, a qual escreveu um livro muito controverso, foi para a África. The sister of my friend, who wrote a very controversial book, has gone to Africa.

If we had used **que** we might be in some doubt as to whether the writer was the friend or the sister. The feminine form **a qual** makes it clear that it is the sister.

The forms **qual** and **quais** are also preceded by prepositions combined with the articles. For example: **do** (etc), **no** (etc), **pelo** (etc).

A praia, pela qual passeámos, tem muitas recordações para mim. The beach, which we walked along, has many memories for me. *See section 10, page 24.*

Exercise 9

Translate the following:
1 Qual é a estação mais próxima daqui?
2 Qual é a sua morada? (Also 'endereço' which is used more in Brazil)
3 Que horas são?
4 Ela nunca faz o que eu quero.
5 Porque não vai de automóvel?
6 Creio que é muito longe.
7 Como vão os seus negócios?
8 Onde vai você?
9 Quando vão eles a Lisboa?
10 Quanto devo?

Vocabulary and key to pronunciation:
estação [ish-te^r-*sah*-oo^n] station
a mais próxima [*mah*-ish *proh*-see-me^r] nearest (*f sing.*)
daqui [de^r-*kee*] to here (from here)
morada [moo-*rah*-de^r] address
horas [*oh*-re^{r}sh] hours, time
nunca [*noo*^{n}-ke^r] never
faz [fahsh] makes, does
quero [*keh*-roo] I want
vai [*vah*-ee] go, goes
automóvel [ah'oo-too-*moh*-vel] car
creio [*kray*-oo] I believe
longe]*lo*^{n}-zh^e] far
vão [*vah*-oo^n] go (*pl*) are going
seus [*say*-oosh] your (*formal pl*)
negócios [n^e-*goh*-see-oosh] business (*pl*)
devo [*deh*-voo] I owe

14 Demonstrative adjectives and pronouns

this	these
este [*aysh*-t^e] *m sing.*	**estes** [*aysh*-t^{e}sh] *m pl*
esta [*esh*-te^r] *f sing.*	**estas** [*esh*-te^{r}sh] *f pl*
isto [*ish*-too] *indeterminate*	

34

that (*near to person addressed*)	those

esse [*ay*-s^e] *m sing.*   **esses** [*ay*-s^{e}sh] *m*
essa [*es*-se^r] *f sing.*   **essas** [*es*-se^{r}sh] *f pl*
isso [*e*-soo] *indeterminate*

that (*over there*)	those

aquele [e^r-*kay*-l^e] *m sing.*   **aqueles** [e^r-*kay*-lesh] *m pl*
aquela [e^r-*keh*-le^r] *f sing.*   **aquelas** [e^r-*keh*-le^{r}sh] *f pl*
aquilo [e^r-*kee*-loo] *indeterminate*

The demonstrative adjectives and pronouns combine with the prepositions **de** and **em**, and the demonstrative adjective **aquele/aquela** also combines with the preposition **a**. For example:

nesta = **em** + **esta** in this, on this, at this (*f sing.*)
daquele = **de** + **aquele** of that (*m sing.*)
àquela = **a** + **aquela** [*ah*-*keh*-le^r] to that, at that (*f sing.*)
isto, isso, aquilo are used in place of nouns, when the gender of noun is not known or indeterminate.

Exercise 10

Translate the following:
1 Aquela loja à esquina.
2 Vamos àquela praia.
3 O que é isto?
4 Isto é um computador.
5 Por favor feche essa porta.
6 Este é o meu marido e aquele é o meu filho.
7 Estas chaves não são minhas.
8 Ele está naquele hotel.
9 Esta mala é daquele senhor.
10 This house is large.
11 What is that? (*closer to the person addressed*)
12 I do not want those (*over there*) books.
13 This is impossible.
14 These men are English.

Vocabulary and key to pronunciation:

praia [*prah*-ye^r] beach
computador [ko^n-poo-te^r-*dor*] computer
feche [*fay*-sh^e] shut (*imperative form*)
meu marido [*may*-oo me^r-*ree*-doo] my husband
filho [*fee*-l'yoo] son

chaves [*shah*-v^{e}sh] keys
minhas [*mee*-n'yersh] mine (*f pl*)
mala [*mah*-le^r] suitcase (*also* handbag)
grande [*gra^n*-d^e] large

CONVERSATION

Um telefonema/a telephone call

Brrr . . . Brrr . . . Brrr . . . Brrr . . .

Maria	Estou.
António	Está lá? É a Maria?
Maria	Sou sim. Quem fala?
António	Daqui fala o António. Bom dia como está?
Maria	Bem, obrigada. E você e sua familia?
António	Menos mal, obrigado. Estou muito cansado. Ontem à noite voltei de Londres.
Maria	E então teve férias boas?
António	Sim, mas o tempo estava péssimo.
Maria	Você fez muitas compras?
António	Não muitas. Está tudo tão caro! Mas comprei uma lembrança para você que, infelizmente, se quebrou na viagem.
Maria	Não faz mal. Você é muito amável. Agradeço-lhe da mesma maneira.
António	Aonde vai passar as férias este ano?
Maria	Estou a pensar em ir a Londres também.
António	Fala Inglês?
Maria	Não muito bem, mas faço-me compreender.
António	Londres é uma grande cidade, e linda, mas está sempre a chover. Você terá de levar um guarda-chuva.
Maria	Claro.
António	Então Maria – que há de novo? E sua irmã Emilia? Que é feito dela?
Maria	Mas eu não tenho nenhuma irmã.
António	Você não se chama Maria dos Anjos da Silva?
Maria	Não, chamo-me Maria da Conceição Lopes.
António	Desculpe, enganei-me no número.

Key to the conversation

Maria	Hello? (*literally* 'I am').
António	Hello? (*literally* 'Are you there?') Is that you Maria?
Maria	Yes, it's me. Who is that speaking?

António	António speaking (*literally* 'from here speaks António'). Good morning, how are you?
Maria	Well, thank you. And you and your family?
António	Not too badly, thank you. I am very tired. Last night (*literally* 'yesterday night') I returned from London.
Maria	And did you have good holidays?
António	Yes, but the weather was awful.
Maria	Did you do much shopping? (*literally* 'purchases')
António	Not much. (*literally* 'not many'). Everything is so expensive! But I bought a gift for you which, unfortunately, has got broken during the trip.
Maria	It doesn't matter. You are very kind. Thank you all the same.
António	Where are you going to spend your holidays this year?
Maria	I am thinking of going to London too.
António	Do you speak English?
Maria	Not very well, but I make myself understood.
António	London is a great city, and beautiful, but it is always raining. You will have to take an umbrella.
Maria	Naturally.
António	Well Maria – what news? (*literally* 'What is there which is new?') And what about your sister Emilia? What has happened to her?
Maria	But I don't have a sister.
António	Are you not (*literally* 'don't you call yourself') Maria dos Anjos da Silva?
Maria	No. My name is (*literally* 'I call myself/I am called') Maria da Conceicao Lopes.
António	Oh I am sorry. I have the wrong number. (*literally* 'I made a mistake in the number').

Please repeat the following expressions from the previous conversation:
Por favour repita as expressões seguintes referentes a conversação anterior:

menos mal [*may*-noosh mahl] not too bad (badly)
ontem à noite [o^n-te^n ah *noy*-t^e] last night (*literally* 'yesterday at night')
então [e^n-*tah*-oo^n] well, well then, so (*frequently used*)
férias boas [*feh*-ree-e^{r}sh *boh*-e^{r}sh] good holidays (or **boas férias**)
infelizmente [een-feh-leesh-*me^n*-te] unfortunately
Não faz mal. [*nah*-oo^n fahsh mahl] It doesn't matter.
É muito amável. [eh *mwee^n*-too e^r-*mah*-vel] You are (*or* he/she is) very kind.
Agradeço-lhe. [e^r-gre^r-*day*-soo-l'y^e] (I) thank you.
da mesma maneira [de^r *maysh*-me^r me^r-*nay*-re^r] all the same, in the same way
este ano [aysh-t'*e^r*-noo]* this year

claro [*klah*-roo] of course, certainly, obviously, it goes without saying, etc
(*very much in use*)
Que há de novo? [kee ah d^e *no*-voo] What is new? What (is the) news?
Que é feito dela? [kee'eh *fay*-too *deh*-le^r] What has happened to her? What
has she been doing?
Enganei-me. [e^n-ge^r-*nay*-m^e] I made a mistake.

*Note that when a word ends in the vowel **e** and the following word begins
with a vowel, the **e** stops being mute and takes on the sound of **ee** adjoining
the following vowel. This is something in Portuguese pronunciation which
the student must be aware of. The words are run together in what sounds
like a very long word. When the word ends in a consonant and the next
starts with a vowel, those two words are also joined in pronunciation, the
final **s** (which normally has the sound of **sh**) taking on the sound of **z**.

Fourth lesson/quarta lição

15 Possessive adjectives and pronouns

| | Thing(s) possessed | | | |
	m sing.	f sing.	m pl	f pl
my, mine	o meu	a minha	os meus	as minhas
your, yours (*familiar*)	o teu	a tua	os teus	as tuas
your, yours (*formal*)	o seu	a sua	os seus	as suas
his/her, hers/its	o seu	a sua	os seus	as suas
our, ours	o nosso	a nossa	os nossos	as nossas
your, yours	o vosso	a vossa	os vossos	as vossas
their, theirs	o seu	a sua	os seus	as suas

Since the forms **seu**, **sua**, **seus**, **suas** mean 'his/her, hers/their, theirs' as well as 'your, yours' (*formal*), to avoid ambiguity the forms **dele**, **dela**, **deles**, **delas** (*literally* 'of him', 'of her', 'of them') are often used instead. For example:

o seu lápis his/her/your pencil. But:
o lápis dele his pencil
o lapis dela her pencil

In the plural:
as suas casas his/her/your/their houses. But:
as casas deles their houses
as casas dela her houses

You will have noticed that the dele, dela, deles, delas forms agree in number and gender with the subject noun ('he', 'she' etc.), also that they come *after* the object ('houses').

The definite article precedes a possessive adjective but it can be left out when speaking of close relatives. It is often omitted in Brazil. The possessive pronouns (mine, etc) do not require an article except when emphasizing ownership.
Unlike English usage, the possessive adjective can be omitted in Portuguese when there is no doubt about the ownership. A common instance is in referring to parts of the body or personal clothing. For example:

39

Vou lavar as mãos. [vo le^r-*vahr* e^{r}sh *mah*-oo^{n}sh] I am going to wash my hands.
Vista o casaco. [*vee*-ste^r oo ke^r-*zah*-koo] Put on your coat.

Exercise 11

Translate the following:
1 Gosto muito da vossa casa.
2 Este é o seu copo e aquele é o dele.
3 A tua filha é muito simpática.
4 As nossas férias começam em Junho.
5 A minha mulher chega sempre atrasada.
6 Are these your suitcases?
7 My telephone is always out of order.
8 This is not mine.
9 I don't know their name.
10 Your (*pl*) house is very far.
11 Our daughter is arriving tomorrow.
12 His friend (*m*) is American.

Vocabulary and key to pronunciation:

gosto de [*goh*'sh-too d^e] I like
copo [*koh*-poo] glass
filha [*feel*-ye^r] daughter
simpática [see^n-*pah*-tee-ke^r] nice, charming
férias [*feh*-ree-e^{r}sh] holidays
começam [koo-*meh*-saw^n] they begin
Junho [*zhoon*-yoo] June
mulher [mool-*yehr*] wife
chega [*shay*-ge^r] arrives
atrasada [e^r-tre^r-*zah*-de^r] late (*f sing.*)
avariado [e^r-ve^r-ree-*ah*-doo] out of order
não sei [*nah*-oo^n say] I don't know
o nome [oo *noh*-me^r] the name
longe [*lo^n*-zh^e] far
amanhã [e^r-*me^{r}n*-yah^n] tomorrow
amigo [e^r-*mee*-goo] friend
americano [e^r-m^e-ree-ke^r-noo] American (*m sing.*)

16 Cardinal numbers

1	um [oo^n] (m)	50	cinquenta [si^n-kwe^n-te^r]
	uma [oo-me^r] (f)	60	sessenta
2	dois [do'ish] (m)	70	setenta
	duas [doo-e^{r}sh] (f)	80	oitenta
3	três [traysh]	90	noventa
4	quatro [kwah-tro]	100	cem [se^n]
5	cinco [see^n-koo]		
6	seis [say'ish]	101	cento e um/uma
7	sete [sett]	102	cento e dois/duas
8	oito [oh'it-too]	120	cento e vinte
9	nove [noh'v^e]	125	cento e vinte e cinco
10	dez [daysh]	200	duzentos [doo-ze^n-toosh] (m)
			duzentas (f)
11	onze [o^{n}z^e]	201	duzentos/as e um/uma
12	doze [dohz^e]	300	trezentos/as
13	treze [tray-z^e]	400	quatrocentos/as
14	catorze [ke^r-tor-z^e]	500	quinhentos/as
15	quinze [keen-z^e]	600	seiscentos/as
16	dezasseis [d^e-ze^r-say'ish]	700	setecentos/as
17	dezassete [d^e-ze^r-sett]	800	oitocentos/as
18	dezoito [d^e-zoh'it-too]	900	novecentos/as
19	dezanove [d^e-ze^r-noh'v^e]	1000	mil [meel]
20	vinte [vee^n-te]		
		1100	mil e cem
21	vinte e um/uma	1101	mil cento e um/uma
22	vinte e dois/duas	2000	dois/duas mil
23	vinte e três	100,000	cem mil
30	trinta [tree^n-te^r]	1,000,000	um milhão [meel-yah-oo^n]
40	quarenta [kwe^r-ren-te^r]	2,000,000	dois milhões

Estamos em mil novecentos e oitenta e dois. We are in 1982.

Quero três selos – um de nove escudos e dois de dez e meio. I would like (I want) three stamps – one of nine escudos and two of 10½ escudos.

O meu pai faz hoje sessenta anos. My father is sixty years old today. (*Note idiomatic use of verb* 'fazer'.)

Os nossos amigos chegam no dia vinte e oito de Maio. Our friends arrive (will arrive) on the 28th of May.

Há dois meses que não como carne. I have not eaten meat for two months. (*Note idiomatic use of* 'Há'. *See section 6, page 16.*)

17 Time/horas

Que horas são? What time is it?

São onze horas em ponto. It is 11 o'clock precisely.

São cinco e dez minutos. It is ten past five.

São oito e meia. It is half past eight.

São duas e vinte e cinco. It is twenty-five past two.

São quatro e um quarto. It is a quarter past four.

São vinte para as seis. It is twenty to six.

Faltam vinte para as seis. A *colloquial expression, literally* 'twenty missing out of six'.

São seis menos vinte. *Literally* 'six less twenty'.

São cinco e quarenta. *Literally* 'five and forty'.

É uma hora. It is one o'clock.

É meio dia. It is mid-day.

É meia noite. It is midnight.

Exercise 12

Translate the following:
1 Acabo o trabalho às seis horas.
2 Vamos passar quinze dias na praia.
3 Ela tem quatro irmãos.
4 O livro custa vinte escudos (20$00).
5 Este elevador leva só cinco pessoas.
6 Vou a Paris de quatro em quatro semanas.
7 He begins his work at 8 o'clock.
8 He has two boys and three girls.
9 I write to my mother every five days.
10 He leaves on the 20th of May.
11 Do you eat at one o'clock?
12 He has not worked for ten days.
13 I am thirty-five years old.
14 It is a quarter to six.

Vocabulary and key to pronunciation:

acabo [e^r-*kah*-boo] I finish
passar [pe^r-*sahr*] to spend
custa [*koosh*-te^r] costs
elevador [ill-ve^r-*dor*] lift, elevator
mãe [mah'e^n] mother

leva [*leh*-ve^r] takes, carries
Paris [pe^r-*reesh*] Paris
de quatro em quatro semanas [s^e-*me*^{r}-ne^{r}sh] every four weeks
começa [koo-*meh*-se^r] begins ·
escrevo [ish-*kre*-voo] I write
trabalha [tre^r-*bahl*-ye^r] he/she works

18 Days of the week/dias da semana

domingo [doo-*mee*^{n}-goo] Sunday
segunda-feira [s^e-*goo*^{n}-de^r *fay*-re^r] Monday
terça-feira [*tayr*-se^r *fay*-re^r] Tuesday
quarta-feira [*kwahr*-te^r] Wednesday
quinta-feira [*kee*^{n}-te^r] Thursday
sexta-feira [*saysh*-te^r] Friday
sábado [*sah*-be^r-doo] Saturday

Hoje é domingo. Today is Sunday.
Amanhã será segunda-feira. Tomorrow will be Monday.
Depois de amanhã será terça-feira. The day after tomorrow will be Tuesday.
Ontem foi sábado. Yesterday was Saturday.
Anteontem (*also:* antes de ontem) foi sexta-feira. The day before yesterday was Friday.

hoje à noite tonight
esta tarde this afternoon
esta manhã this morning
amanhã de manhã tomorrow morning
amanhã à noite tomorrow evening/night
daqui a quinze dias in a fortnight's time
na próxima semana next week (*also:* na semana que vem)
no mês passado last month
véspera the day before

19 Months of the year/meses do ano

Janeiro [zhe^r-*nare*-roo] January
Fevereiro [f^{e}v-*rare*-roo] February
Março [*mahr*-soo] March
Abril [e^r-*breel*] April
Maio [*mah*-yoo] May
Junho [*zhoon*-yoo] June

Julho [*zhool*-yoo] July
Agosto [e^r-*goh*'stoo] August
Setembro [s^e-*te*^{n}-broo] September
Outubro [oh-*too*-broo] October
Novembro [noo-*ve*^{n}-broo] November
Dezembro [d^e-*ze*^{n}-broo] December

20 Seasons of the year/estações do ano

a Primavera [e^r pree-me^r-*veh*-re^r] spring
o Verão [oo v^e-*rah*'oo^n] summer
o Outono [oo oh-*toh*-noo] autumn
o Inverno [oo ee^n-*vehr*-noo] winter
a Consoada Christmas Eve
o Natal Christmas
Feliz Natal Happy Christmas
a Véspera do Ano Novo New Year's Eve
Ano Novo New Year
Próspero Ano Novo Happy New Year
a Quaresma Lent
a Páscoa Easter
Páscoa feliz Happy Easter

In Brazil, months and seasons are written with small initial letters.

Exercise 13
Translate the following:
1 Na próxima semana vou a casa da minha tia.
2 No mês passado o meu irmão foi para o Brasil trabalhar.
3 Os meus filhos chegam daqui a quinze dias.
4 Hoje à noite vamos ao teatro.
5 A primavera é a minha estação favorita.
6 Ontem esteve muito frio.
7 Depois de amanhã temos os resultados dos nossos exames.
8 I am going to spend Christmas with my friends in Lisbon.
9 This year I have no holidays.
10 She is going to spend summer in the Algarve.
11 Yesterday was hot.
12 My birthday is on Sunday.
13 Tomorrow morning I begin work.
14 July, August and September are very hot months in Portugal.

Vocabulary and key to pronunciation:
foi [foh'^{e}] went
vamos [*ve^r*-moosh] we are going
esteve [ish-*tay*-v^e] was
fez [faysh] made/did
passar [pe^r-*sahr*] to spend time
férias [*feh*-re-e^{r}sh] holidays
faço [*fah*-soo] I do/make
começo [koo-*meh*-soo] I begin
meses quentes [*may*-z^{e}sh *ke^n*-t^{e}sh] hot months

CONVERSATIONAL SENTENCES

1
A Desculpe. Dizia-me por favor que horas são?
B Desculpe, mas não lhe posso dizer as horas, porque o meu relógio está parado. Mas, oiça – parece-me que o relógio da catedral está a dar horas.
A Tem razão. Está, na verdade, a dar horas. São três horas.

2
A Estou muito preocupada.
B Então porquê?
A Já são seis e vinte e o meu marido ainda não chegou. Está sempre atrasado.
B Não estou de acordo. No meu relógio tenho seis e um quarto. O seu relógio deve estar adiantado.
A Não pode ser; o meu relógio está sempre certo. Além disso ouvi, ainda há pouco, as notícias das dezóito horas (18.00).
B Nesse caso é o meu que não está a trabalhar bem. Mas, quanto ao seu marido – não se esqueça que é a hora de ponta* e que é sexta-feira.
A Já se faz tarde para o teatro. Há que tempos que eu ando a tentar arranjar bilhetes. Finalmente consegui. Mas, esta noite o espectáculo começa às sete e quinze.
B Ainda tem tempo. Olhe, aqui vem o seu marido.
A Ainda bem!

3
A Você acha que faz calor demais no Algarve em Junho?
B Não. Creio que ainda é suportável, e as praias não têm tanta gente como nos outros meses do Verão. Eu confesso que prefiro ir para o Sul da Europa no Outono. Não aguento o calor. E em Outubro e Novembro ainda há muito sol em Portugal mas não faz tanto calor.
A Eu só posso ter férias em Junho; e além disso dou-me muito bem com o calor. Detesto a chuva, o vento e o frio.
B Eu também.

*In Brazil: a hora do 'rush'

Key to the conversational sentences:

1
A Excuse me. Would you please tell me what time it is?
B I am sorry, but I cannot tell you the time because my watch has stopped. But listen – I believe that (*literally* it seems to me that) the cathedral clock is striking.
A You are right. It is indeed striking. It is three o'clock.

2
A I am very worried.
B Yes, why?

A It is already twenty past six and my husband has not arrived yet. He is always late.
B I do not agree. My watch says (*literally* on my watch I have) a quarter past six. Your watch must be fast.
A It can't be. My watch is always right. Besides, I heard the six o'clock news on the radio a while ago.
B In that case, it is mine that is not working (well). But, about your husband – don't forget it's the rush hour and that it's Friday.
A It's getting late for the theatre. I have been trying to get tickets for ages. Finally I got them (*literally* I succeeded). But tonight the show starts at 7.15.
B You still have time. Look – here comes your husband.
A Just as well! (Thank goodness!)

3

A Do you think it is too hot in the Algarve in June?
B No. I believe that it is still bearable, and the beaches do not have as many people as in the other summer months. I must say (I confess) I prefer to go to the south of Europe in the autumn. I cannot bear the heat. And in October and November it is still very sunny in Portugal (*literally* there is still much sun), but it is not so hot (*literally* it does not do so much heat).
A I can only have (my) holidays in June; and besides I like (*literally* I get on with) the heat. I hate the rain, wind and cold.
B Me too. (So do I.)

Please repeat the following expressions:
Por favor repita as seguintes expressões:

1
dizia-me [dee-*zee*'e^r-m^e] would you tell me?/did you tell me?/were you telling me? (*This is the imperfect tense of the verb* **dizer** [dee-*zayr*] *to say, to tell. In Portuguese this tense is often used instead of the conditional.*)
oiça [*oh*'e-se^r] listen/hear (*imperative form of the verb* **ouvir** to hear)
parece-me [pe^r-*reh*-s^e-m^e] it seems to me, it appears
dar horas [dahr *oh*-re^{r}sh] to strike the hour (*literally* to give hours)
na verdade [ne^r v^{e}r-*dah*-d^e] indeed, in fact, in truth

2
estou muito preocupada [pry'oh-koo-*pah*-de^r] I am very worried
ainda não chegou [*sh^e*-go] not yet arrived
estou de acordo [ish-*toh* de^r-*kohr*-doo] I agree
não pode ser it cannot be
além disso [ah-*le^n dee*-soo] besides that, besides
ainda há pouco [e^r-*ee^n*-de^r ah *po*-koo] a while ago
nesse caso [*neh*-s^e *kah*-zoo] in that case
quanto a as to, as for, regarding, speaking of
não se esqueça [*nah*'oo^n s'ish-*keh*-se^r] do not forget

hora de ponta/hora de movimento [po^n-te^r/moo-vee-me^n-too] rush hour
já se faz tarde [zhah s^e fahsh tar-d^e] it is becoming late
há que tempos [ah k^e te^n-posh] for ages
ando a tentar I have been trying (*present of verb* **andar** to walk/to move/to be)
ainda tem tempo you still have time, you are still in time
ainda bem thank goodness

3
não aguento [e^r-gwe^n-too], **não suporto** [soo-$pohr$-to] I can't bear, I can't stand
dou-me muito bem com [do-me moo'i^n-too be^n] I get on very well with, in
posso [$poss$-soo] I can
eu também so do I

Other vocabulary:

relógio [r^e-loh-zhe'oo] watch, clock
atrasado [e^r-tre^r-zah-doo] slow, late
adiantado [e^r-dy'a^n-tah-doo] fast
certo [$sehr$-too] right, correct
arranjar [e^r-ra^n-jahr] to get, obtain, arrange
bilhetes [bee-yeh-t^{e}sh] tickets
finalmente [fee-nahl-me^n-t^e] finally, at last
consegui *past tense of verb* **conseguir** to succeed, to manage, to achieve, to be able to
espectáculo [ish-peh-tah-koo-loo] show
acha? [ah-she^r] do you think?
gente* [zhe^n-t^e] people

(*Note that **gente** is singular in form and requires a singular verb although it is translated by an English plural, 'people'. For example: **a gente é** = the people *are*. Colloquially, **gente** + 3rd person singular of the verb has come to mean 'we'. Thus, **a gente é** = **nós somos**.)

From now on, there will not be a full translation of the conversational matter; only repetition and translation of new expressions and words. The imitated pronunciation will also be discontinued; if you are still having difficulty with this aspect of the language, our cassette recordings of the text will help considerably.

Fifth lesson/quinta lição

21 The feminine forms of adjectives and nouns

As we have seen in lesson 1, nouns and adjectives are either masculine or feminine. We have learnt how to identify them and change from one gender to the other where applicable. For example:

o gato, a gata cat
o velho, a velha old man, old woman
António, Antónia
pintor, pintora painter
francês, francesa French
espanhol, espanhola Spanish
alemão, alemã German

And now that you have a clear picture, we add a little spice. There are nouns ending in **a** which are masculine. They are Greek derivatives mainly. For example:

o tema the theme
o sistema the system
o clima the climate
o telefonema, the telephone call
o quilograma the kilo
o panorama the panorama, view
o poeta the poet
o dia the day
o mapa the map

But the noun **criança** ('child') is always preceded by the article in the feminine (**a criança**) and refers to both sexes.

Nouns and adjectives ending in **e**, in general do not alter; only the preceding article changes according to the gender. For example:

o estudante, a estudante the student *m* & *f*
o lápis verde the green pencil
a caneta verde the green pen
um quarto grande a large bedroom
uma sala grande a large sitting-room

But **gente** (people) is always preceded by the article in the feminine.

Nouns and adjectives ending in **-ista** refer to both genders but their preceding article changes accordingly. For example:

o pianista, a pianista male pianist, female pianist
o artista, a artista performer
o telefonista, a telefonista switchboard/telephone operator
o vigarista, a vigarista crook, swindler
comunista, fascista etc

Adjectives ending in a consonant generally remain unchanged:

um homem agradável a pleasant man;
uma mulher agradável a pleasant woman
o rapaz está feliz the boy is happy;
a rapariga está feliz the girl is happy
o Mercado Comum the Common Market;
uma casa comum a common house
uma lição simples an easy lesson;
um caso simples a simple case

-eu usually changes to **-eia**. For example: **Europeu, Europeia**

Some nouns ending in **-or** usually change to **-riz**. For example: **actor, actriz, embaixador, embaixatriz**

Some words ending in **-u** (not **-eu**) become feminine by adding **a**. For example: **cru, crua** raw

Irregular adjectives:
mau, má bad (*m & f*)
bom, boa good (*m & f*)

Numeral **dois** (*m*), **duas** (*f*) two
Also, **o poeta** (poet) becomes **a poetisa** (poetess)

Exercise 14

Fill in the blanks:
1 Hoje o tempo está ____. (bad)
2 Ela é uma ____ ____. (good secretary)
3 Não sei onde está ____ ____ ____ ____. (my French map)
4 ____ ____ (My sister) é mais ____ (old) do que eu.
5 ____ ____ ____ (My friend, *f*) é ____ (Spanish) mas o marido dela é ____. (English)
6 É uma ____ ____ (good thing) que você faz.
7 Há ____ ____ ____ (many pleasant people) neste mundo.
8 O meu colega está muito ____ (happy) no Brasil.

9 O Mercado Comum é uma comunidade ____. (European)
10 A mãe da minha amiga é ____ ____. (a poet)
11 Tenho um ____ ____ ____. (large green car)
12 Meu primo é um ____ ____ (good writer) e a mulher dele é tambem ____ ____ ____. (writer)
13 O António é um ____ ____. (Portuguese journalist)
14 Esta galinha está ____. (uncooked)

Vocabulary:

tempo weather
não sei I don't know
coisa thing
neste mundo in this world

comunidade community
jornalista journalist
galinha chicken
escritor writer

22 Plural of nouns and adjectives

As seen in lesson 1, the general rule is to add an s to nouns and adjectives ending in a vowel in order to form the plural, and es to those that end in r, s, z. For example:

casa becomes casas
amante becomes amantes (lovers)

feliz becomes felizes
flor becomes flores

But nouns and adjectives ending in m change m to ns in the plural. For example:

o homem becomes os homens (the man, the men)
a viagem becomes as viagens (the journey, the journeys)

Nouns and adjectives ending in -al, -el, -ol, -ul change l to is in the plural. For example:

a capital becomes as capitais
espanhol becomes espanhóis

o papel becomes os papéis
azul becomes azuis (blue)

Those ending in -il form their plural in two different ways, depending on whether the -il is stressed or not.
Stressed -il is changed to -is. For example: civil becomes civis
Unstressed -il is changed to -eis. For example: fácil becomes fáceis

Nouns and adjectives ending in -ão form the plural in one of three ways, as follows:

-ão to -ões This is the most commonly found method of changing -ão words into the plural. For example:

o limão lemon, becomes os limões
a lição lesson, becomes as lições
o leão lion, becomes os leões

-ão to -ães There are four words in common use which exhibit this method of changing. They are given below and can be easily memorized:

o capitão captain, becomes os capitães
o alemão German, becomes os alemães
o cão dog, becomes os cães
o pão loaf of bread, becomes os pães

-ão to -ãos There are very few examples of this type. The most important are the following:

o irmão brother, becomes os irmãos
a mão hand, becomes as mãos
o cristão Christian, becomes os cristãos
o órfão orphan, becomes os órfãos
o cidadão citizen, becomes os cidadãos (*also:* cidadães)

Note that in Portuguese, a masculine plural can include both sexes. For example, **pais** can mean 'fathers', but frequently means 'parents'. Similarly, **filhos** can mean 'sons' but also means 'children'. **Tios** can mean 'uncles' but also 'uncle and aunt', and so on.

Exercise 15

Translate the following:
1 Two sitting-rooms.
2 My brother and sister.
3 The flowers are beautiful.
4 These problems are difficult.
5 In the summer, there are many people on the beaches.
6 Three English students.
7 Four sheets.
8 My friends (*m* & *f*) are very kind.
9 I do not know these men.
10 The German children do not like the dogs.
11 I buy five loaves of bread every day.
12 She likes all animals.
13 My sister has blue eyes.
14 I have dirty hands.
15 (The) lemons are good for your health.
16 My parents are always so happy.

Vocabulary:
sala/sala de estar sitting room
linda pretty, beautiful
problema problem

lençol sheet
amável kind
não conheço I do not know
crianças (f) children
todos all
olhos eyes
sujas dirty
saúde health
tão so, as
gostar de to like

23 The past definite (also known as the preterite or simple past tense)

The past definite ('I spoke', 'I have spoken', 'I did speak') of the three regular conjugations is formed by adding the following terminations (shown in bold type) to the stem of the verb:

	falar (to speak)	**comer** (to eat)	**abrir** (to open)
eu	fal**ei**	com**i**	abr**i**
tu	fal**aste**	com**este**	abr**iste**
ele, ela, você	fal**ou**	com**eu**	abr**iu**
nós	fal**ámos**	com**emos**	abr**imos**
eles, vocês	fal**aram**	com**eram**	abr**iram**

Exercise 16

1 Ontem recebi uma carta da minha amiga.
2 Nós gostámos muito da sua casa.
3 Na semana passada visitámos uma escola muito moderna.
4 Eles partiram para o Brasil.
5 Vocês já venderam a vossa casa?
6 Não, ainda não vendemos a nossa casa.
7 Eles ainda não escreveram.
8 I did not understand.
9 What did they drink?
10 I have already eaten.
11 When did they leave?
12 At what time did the train leave?
13 We did not open the window.
14 He did not eat last night.
15 Did you (*informal*) speak to your mother?
16 I met (knew)* your brother in Lisbon.

Vocabulary:

beber to drink
já already
a que horas at what time
chegar to arrive
janela window
ontem à noite last night
mãe mother
conhecer* to know
Lisboa Lisbon

*The verb **conhecer** – to know – is used in Portuguese to express the English verb 'to meet' in situations where it means 'to meet someone for the first time' – on being introduced, for example. In other situations, the verb 'to meet' is normally **encontrar**.

24 Polite form of the imperative

This is in fact the subjunctive mood

Regular verbs

	falar to speak	**comer** to eat	**abrir** to open
singular	Fale Speak!	Coma Eat!	Abra Open!
plural	Falem Speak!	Comam Eat!	Abram Open!
Let us . . .	Falemos	Comamos	Abramos

The true Portuguese imperative has in fact only two persons; **tu** (you *familiar*) and **vôs** (you *pl formal*):

falar	**comer**	**abrir**
fala	come	abre
falai	comei	abri

In the negative form as well as in the polite form, the subjunctive mood is used as shown above. See the Appendix (verb table) page 135.

Irregular verbs

With certain exceptions (*see* Appendix, page 135), the polite imperative of irregular verbs is formed from the stem of the first person singular of the present indicative plus the endings shown in bold in the following table of common irregular verbs:

	ver to see	trazer to bring	fazer to do, to make	dar to give
singular	Veja See!	Traga	Faça	Dê
plural	Vejam See!	Tragam	Façam	Dêem
Let us ...	Vejamos	Tragamos	Façamos	Dêmos

	dizer to say	ser to be	estar to be	querer to want
singular	Diga	Seja	Esteja	Queira
plural	Digam	Sejam	Estejam	Queiram
Let us ...	Digamos	Sejamos	Estejamos	Queiramos

	ter to have	vir to come	ir to go	pôr to put
singular	Tenha	Venha	Vá	Ponha
plural	Tenham	Venham	Vão	Ponham
Let us ...	Tenhamos	Venhamos	Vamos	Ponhamos

Exercise 17

1 Venha cá.
2 Fale devagar.
3 Não faça barulho.
4 Vá por ali.
5 Não seja tonto.
6 Esteja quieto.
7 Traga a lista dos vinhos.
8 Speak slowly.
9 Let us open the window.
10 Shut (*pl*) the door.
11 Do not eat (*pl*) so quickly.
12 Let us see . . .
13 Come (*pl*) at once.
14 Let us go.
15 Do not speak (*pl*) so loudly.
16 Don't say anything.

Vocabulary:

cá here
devagar slowly
barulho noise
por ali that way, over there
tonto silly
quieto still
lista de vinhos wine list
fechar to close

tão depressa as quickly
já already, at once, straight away
nada nothing, anything
ali there
por ali over there, that way, through there
alto loud, loudly, high, tall

CONVERSATION

Um emprego em Moçambique/a job in Mozambique

Luisa A sua irmã Ann sempre conseguiu o tal emprego em
      Moçambique?
Jane   Sim, recebeu a resposta há duas semanas, depois de muitas
      entrevistas e de esperar seis meses. Está nas suas sete quintas,
      porque já desesperava de ser aceite. O ordenado é bom, mas o que
      mais lhe agrada é a oportunidade de conhecer um país do 'terceiro
      mundo'.
Luisa Que género de trabalho é? Não me lembro do que ela me disse.
Jane   Ela vai ensinar matemática numa escola secundária.
      Aparentemente há lá falta de professores. Já está tudo arranjado.
      Só falta o visto. Você sabe que ela vai primeiro a Lisboa por dois
      meses em curso de férias, com todas as despesas pagas?
Luisa Não, não sabia nada disto. Que bom! E que sorte!
Jane   É verdade. Tanto mais que o noivo também tem esperanças de ir
      para lá. Precisam de engenheiros civis. Ele respondeu a um
      anúncio e agora está à espera de resposta. Tanto ele como a Ann
      querem conhecer a África.
Luisa Mas ele fala português?
Jane   Fala sim, e fluentemente. Ele tirou um curso de Português há anos,
      e depois esteve a trabalhar em Lisboa, uns anos.
Luisa E quando se casam?
Jane   Tencionam casar-se daqui a dois anos se tudo correr bem.
Luisa Quando parte a Ann para Lisboa?
Jane   Na próxima quinta-feira, no voo da TAP. Oxalá não haja nevoeiro
      ou gréves.
Luisa Vou telefonar-lhe esta noite a desejar-lhe boa sorte. Adeus, até à
      vista.

Vocabulary:

tal such, that, the said . . .
receber to receive
conseguir to get, to obtain
conseguir + *infinitive* = to manage to . . ., to succeed in . . .

sempre always, after all, in the end
sempre conseguiu (*idiomatic use of* sempre) she obtained in the end
responder to reply
resposta an answer, a reply
há duas semanas two weeks ago; **há anos** years ago (*see idiomatic uses of* haver *in section 6, page 16*)
depois de after
entrevista interview
quinta farm
Está nas suas sete quintas. (*idiomatic expression*) She is in her seventh heaven. She is over the moon. (*literally* She is in her seven farms.)
desesperar de to despair, to give up hope of
aceitar to accept
ser aceite to be accepted
ordenado salary
agradar to please
o que mais lhe agrada . . . what pleases her most . . .
terceiro mundo third world
género type, kind
lembrar-se de to remember
ensinar to teach
escola secundária secondary school
faltar to be lacking, to be missing
falta shortage
Há lá falta. There is a shortage over there.
arranjar to arrange
Já está tudo arranjado. Everything is already arranged.
visto visa
curso de férias summer (holiday) course
despesas expenses
todas as despesas pagas all expenses paid
saber to know
Não sabia nada disto. I didn't know anything about it.
Que bom! How marvellous!
verdade truth
É verdade. That's right. That's so.
tanto mais besides, moreover, particularly as
noivo fiancé, bridegroom; **noiva** fiancée, bride
esperança hope
precisar de to need
engenheiros civis civil engineers
anúncio advertisement
Tanto ele como a Ann . . . Both he and Ann . . .
uns anos a few years, for a few years (*see uses of the indefinite article in section 3, page 14*)
tencionar + *infinitive* to intend to

casar-se to marry, to get married
daqui a dois anos in two years from now
correr to go, to proceed, to run
se tudo correr bem if all goes well
voo flight
Oxalá . . . Oxalá não . . . I do hope . . . I hope not . . . *This idiomatic expression derives from the Arabic* Insh' Allah, *meaning 'God willing'.*
nevoeiro fog
greve strike
desejar to wish
Adeus Goodbye
Até à vista. 'Bye for now, see you, *etc*

Sixth lesson/sexta licão

25 Personal pronouns – direct object, indirect object and reflexive form

SINGULAR	*Direct object*	*Indirect object*	*Reflexive*
1st pers.	**me** me	**me** to, for me	**me** myself
2nd person familiar	**te** you	**te** to, for you	**te** yourself
2nd person formal	**o** you (*m*)	**lhe** to, for you (*m*)	**se** yourself (*m*)
	a you (*f*)	**lhe** to, for you (*f*)	**se** yourself (*f*)
3rd person	**o** him, it (*m*)	**lhe** to, for him, it (*m*)	**se** himself, itself (*m*)
	a her, it (*f*)	**lhe** to, for her, it (*f*)	**se** herself, itself (*f*)

PLURAL			
1st person	**nos** us	**nos** to, for us	**nos** ourselves
2nd person familiar	**vos** you	**vos** to, for you	**vos** yourselves
2nd person formal	**os** you (*m*)	**lhes** to, for you (*m*)	**se** yourselves (*m*)
	as you (*f*)	**lhes** to, for you (*f*)	**se** yourselves (*f*)
3rd person	**os** them (*m*)	**lhes** to, for them (*m*)	**se** themselves (*m*)
	as them (*f*)	**lhes** to, for them (*f*)	**se** themselves (f)

Note that in the 3rd person (and therefore in the 2nd person formal), the direct object **o, a, os, as**, is different from the indirect object **lhe, lhes**, and from the reflexive pronoun **se**. In all other cases, however, the object and reflexive pronouns share the same forms.

Combined forms

The direct object pronoun combines with the indirect object pronoun to give the following compounds. Note that the indirect object pronoun always comes first, but number and gender are determined by the direct object.

me ⎫		mo, ma, mos, mas
te ⎬		to, ta, tos, tas
lhe ⎭		lho, lha, lhos, lhas
	plus **o, a, os, as** gives	
nos ⎫		no-lo, no-la, no-los, no-las
vos ⎬		vo-lo, vo-la, vo-los, vo-las
lhes ⎭		lho, lha, lhos, lhas

In the 1st and 2nd persons plural, the **s** of **nos** and **vos** is omitted and replaced by a hyphen before another pronoun. However, the combined forms **no-lo** etc, and **vo-lo** etc, are seldom used in conversation.

These combined forms are often used with the verbs **dar** to give, **trazer** to bring, and **oferecer** to offer. For example:

Dou-lhe a minha morada. I give my address to him.
Dou-lha. I give him/her/you it. [i.e. **morada** (f)]

Word order

In affirmative main sentences, the object pronouns follow the verb and are joined to it by a hyphen. But there are certain circumstances in which they precede the verb, as follows:

1 *In negative sentences*

Não o vejo. I don't see him/you (*m formal*)

2 *In questions*

Porque não nos fala? Why don't you (*formal*) speak to us?

3 *After some prepositions, conjunctions and adverbs*

Sempre me detestou. He/she/you (*formal*) always hated me.
Depois de lhe dar a receita . . . After giving him/her/you (*formal*) the prescription . . .
Antes que me esqueça . . . Before I forget . . .
Eles mal me falam. They hardly speak to me.

Note that the verb **esquecer-se** (to forget) is reflexive in Portuguese.

3rd person pronouns after verbs ending in **r**, **s** and **z**

When a verb ends in *r*, *s* or *z*, the last letter is dropped before the 3rd person pronouns **o, a, os, as**. The letter *l* is then prefixed to the pronoun which is joined to the verb by a hyphen. The affected verbal forms will then be stressed, with an acute accent over the letter *a* and a circumflex over *e* and *o*. The following examples illustrate this point:

Eu quero ver o António. I want to see Anthony.
Eu quero vê-lo. I want to see him.

Eu desejo comprar uvas. I want to buy grapes.
Eu desejo comprá-las. I want to buy them.

Ela faz cestos. She makes baskets.
Ela fá-los. She makes them.

Nós vemos a sua amiga muitas vezes. We often see your friend.
Nós vemo-la muitas vezes. We often see her.

3rd person pronouns after verbs ending in **m**, **ão** and **õe**

When the pronouns **o**, **a**, **os**, **as**, come immediately after a verb ending in *m*, *ão*, or *õe*, the letter *n* is prefixed to the pronoun to give the forms **no**, **na**, **nos**, **nas**, which are then joined to the verb by a hyphen as shown in the following examples:

Eles dão lições ao ar livre. They give lessons in the open air.
Eles dão-nas ao ar livre. They give them in the open air.

Elas viram o irmão da Maria. They saw Maria's brother.
Elas viram-no. They saw him.

Ela põe a mesa. She sets the table.
Ela põe-na. She sets it.

Note that the rule governing the position of object pronouns in negative and interrogative sentences still applies. For example:

Elas não o viram. They didn't see him.
Ela a põe? Is she setting it?

Word order in Brazil

In Brazilian Portuguese, the personal object pronouns nearly always come before the verb. Therefore in Brazil, the word order in the above examples would be:

Eles as dão ao ar livre.
Elas o viram.
Ela a põe.

The reflexive pronoun also comes before the verb. For example:

Eu me sinto cansada. I (*f*) feel tired.
In Portugal: Eu sinto-me cansada.

Disjunctive pronouns

When object pronouns come after prepositions, they are different from the normal object pronouns. This is shown in the table below.

SINGULAR

1st person	**mim** me
2nd person familiar	**ti** you
2nd person formal	**si*, você, o senhor, a senhora** you
3rd person	**ele** him, **ela** her

PLURAL

1st person	**nós** us
2nd person formal	**vós, vocês** (*more casual*), **os senhores, as senhoras** you
3rd person	**eles, elas** them

* In addition to its translation of 'you', **si** can also mean him/herself, themselves. For example:

Ele fala de si para si. He is speaking to himself.

The following examples illustrate the use of the disjunctive pronouns after prepositions:

Este livro é para mim. This book is for me.
Ele gosta de ti. He likes you (*familiar*).
Gosto dela. I like her.
Eu paguei por ela. I paid for her.
Eu acredito em si. I believe you. I believe in you (*formal*).

Some adverbs and prepositions commonly followed by the disjunctive pronoun:

atrás de behind	**contra** against
perto de near	**sem** without
longe de far from	**entre** between, among
em frente de in front of	**antes de** before
em cima de on, on top of	**depois de** after
por baixo de under, below	

The disjunctive pronouns are especially useful for avoiding the ambiguities to which the combined forms frequently give rise. For this reason, the disjunctive forms are much more common in speech. For example:

Dei-lhes o lápis I gave them the pencil, *becomes*
Dei-o a eles *in preference to* **Dei-lho.**

com – *an exception*

The preposition **com** meaning 'with' combines with the disjunctive pronouns **mim, ti, si, nos** and **vos** to give the following special forms:

SINGULAR

com + mim = comigo with me
com + ti = contigo with you (*familiar*)
com + si = consigo with you (*formal*). *Also*: with himself/herself/oneself

PLURAL

com + nos = connosco with us
com + vos = convosco with you

The other disjunctive prepositions require no special change after **com**.

Exercise 18

Translate the following:
1 Dê-lhe os meus cumprimentos.
2 Ela telefonou-me ontem à noite.
3 Viu-o na semana passada.
4 Não as conheço bem.
5 Eles visitam-nos todos os anos.
6 Queremos vê-lo.
7 Vou ajudá-la.
8 Vocês ajudam-no muito.
9 Ele não quer as maçãs, mas eu vou dar-lhas.
10 Você mora perto de mim.
11 Não como sem você.
12 Venha comigo agora tomar um café e depois eu vou consigo ao cabeleireiro.
13 Os cães estão connosco, mas os gatos estão com elas.
14 Quem lho disse?

Vocabulary:

dê (dar) give
cumprimentos regards (best regards)
telefonar to telephone
viu *past definite of* **ver** to see
conhecer to know, to be acquainted with
visitar to visit
querer to want
ajudar to help
depois after, afterwards, then

cabeleireiro hairdresser
cães dogs (*see section 22, page 49*)
gatos cats
disse *past definite of verb* **dizer** to say, to tell.

Omission of the 3rd person pronoun referring to 'things'

When the pronoun corresponds to an inanimate object or an abstract idea and comes at the end of a phrase or sentence, it is often omitted, as the following examples show.

Você viu o filme, 'E tudo o vento levou'? Have you seen the film, 'Gone with the Wind'?
Sim, vi. Yes, I have seen it.

O senhor come carne? Do you eat meat?
Sim, como. Yes, I eat it.

Gosta de Portugal? Do you like Portugal?
Sim, gosto. Yes, I like it.

Vocês beberam o vinho? Did you drink the wine?
Sim, bebemos. Yes, we drank it.

Exercise 19

Translate the following:
1 Show us what you found.
2 Go and look for her.
3 Are these flowers for me?
4 Before I forget, I have to tell you (*pl*).
5 He waited for us.
6 Come with me.
7 There are no secrets between us.
8 I am counting on you (*familiar*).
9 He did not lend it to me.
10 They help him.
11 My mother did not ring me up.
12 I don't need him.
13 I called him but he did not hear me.
14 I saw them (*m*) last week.
15 He is going to see her.

Vocabulary:

mostrar to show
procurar to look for (*in Brazil*: **buscar**)

esperar to wait
segredos secrets
contar com to count on, to count with
emprestar to lend
ajudar to help
telefonar to telephone, to ring up
precisar de to need
chamar to call
ouvir to hear
vi I saw (*past tense of verb* ver)

26 Meals/Refeições

o pequeno-almoço breakfast (*in Brazil:* café da manhã)
o almoço lunch
o lanche tea-time; *also* a merenda
o jantar dinner
a ceia supper

and their respective verbs:

tomar pequeno-almoço to take breakfast
almoçar to take lunch
lanchar to take mid-afternoon tea
jantar to dine

27 The imperfect tense

This is the tense used to express what was happening or used to happen in the past – *during* the past. In the *imperfect* the action is *incomplete* or *interrupted*, unlike the past definite. It is also the tense of description in the past. It is one of the easiest tenses to conjugate, since all verbs (regular and irregular) will have the same ending, depending on which of two groups they belong to.
The first group consists of all verbs ending in -ar. In this group, the imperfect tense ends in -ava etc. The second group consists of verbs ending in -er and -ir. In this group, the imperfect ends in -ia etc.

There are only four exceptions:
tinha (verb ter to have)
vinha (verb vir to come)
punha (verb pôr to put)
era (verb ser to be)

The imperfect is frequently used in place of the conditional. For example:

Gostava de ter . . . I would like to have . . . (conditional **gostaria**) (See also section 32, page 73.)

'I did not know that . . .' or 'I did not know whether . . .' is rendered in the imperfect: **Não sabia que** . . . or **Não sabia se** . . .

The imperfect or past continuous

	falar (to speak)	**comer** (to eat)	**abrir** (to open)
eu	fal**ava**	com**ia**	abr**ia**
tu	fal**avas**	com**ias**	abr**ias**
você	fal**ava**	com**ia**	abr**ia**
ele, ela	fal**ava**	com**ia**	abr**ia**
nós	fal**ávamos**	com**íamos**	abr**íamos**
vocês	fal**avam**	com**iam**	abr**iam**
eles, elas	fal**avam**	com**iam**	abr**iam**

Sentences illustrating the imperfect tense:

Era uma vez . . . Once upon a time . . .

Não sabia* se vinham. I did not know whether they were coming.

Estava ao telefone quando ele entrou. I was on the phone when he came in. ('He came in' is the past definite as his action is complete; mine, on the other hand, was interrupted.)

Quando era pequena, brincava** com as tuas bonecas. When I was a child I played (used to play) with your dolls.

Ela jogava ténis todas as manhãs. She played tennis every morning. (habitual action)

Conhecia-os* bem há muito tempo. I used to know them well a long time ago.

But notice the past definite: **Conheci-os o ano passado.** I met them last year. (See section 23 on page 51.)

Ela nunca comia bolos. She never used to eat cakes.

But:
Ela nunca comeu bolos. She has never eaten cakes.

***Conhecer** to know (= to be acquainted with) can also be translated by 'to meet' (= for the first time), and **soube** – the past definite of **saber** to know

(= knowledge) – is often translated by 'I heard' or 'I learnt'. In English we say 'Can you swim?' but in Portuguese **Sabe nadar?** (= 'do you know how to swim?'); if you were to say **Pode?** ('can you?') it would imply that you had permission to do so, for **Não posso nadar** means 'I am not allowed to swim' (or that I cannot, due to some physical condition). It does not mean that I don't know how to swim.

Note that 'to play' has three translations in Portuguese: **brincar, to play with toys, children, animals, children's games (and it also means 'to tease'); **jogar**, to play games or sport; **tocar**, to play music, bells (it also means 'to touch').

Exercise 20

Translate the following:
1 Quando era criança aprendia tudo mais facilmente.
2 Eu antes comia muito, mas agora não.
3 Íamos todos os dias à praia.
4 Ontem fomos ao campo.
5 Era debaixo desta árvore que eu costumava sentar-me.
6 Que estava você a fazer?
7 Eu estava a tomar banho.
8 What time did you take your breakfast?
9 Would you please tell me where the bus-stop is?
10 I learned that your brother was going to Africa. Is it true?
11 It was raining cats and dogs when we went out.
12 He was listening while I was speaking.
13 I was already eating.
14 Last night I had dinner (dined) with my mother-in-law.

Vocabulary:

aprender to learn
tudo everything
facilmente easily
antes before
agora não not now
fomos we went (*past definite of the verb* **ir**)
campo country, countryside, (*also* a field)
debaixo under, underneath
costumava I used to, I was in the habit of
sentar-se to sit down
a tomar banho to take a bath
paragem do autocarro bus-stop
É verdade? Is it true?
chover to rain
a cântaros (raining) 'cats and dogs'

enquanto while
sair to go out
ouvir to listen
ontem à noite last night
sogra mother-in-law

Translations of 'take'

As the student has no doubt noticed, 'to take' can be translated by several different verbs in Portuguese:

tomar to take (in all senses) food, drink; to seize, grasp something into one's hands; bus, train, bath

levar to take (in the sense of 'to carry' and relating to time)
Levo estas malas comigo. I am taking these suitcases with me.
O avião leva duas horas daqui para Lisboa. The plane takes two hours from here to Lisbon.

tirar to take away, out from, to steal, to take off (removing)
Ele tirou o casaco. He took his coat off.
Ela tirou-me a escova do cabelo. She took my hair brush away.
Você tira muito boas fotografias. You take very good photos.

But:
O avião levanta voo. The plane takes off.

CONVERSATION

Um dia de anos/a birthday

Antónia O domingo passado foi o dia dos anos do meu sogro. Foi uma grande festa. Estava lá, praticamente, toda a família: os sobrinhos americanos do meu sogro, a tia do meu marido que veio do Brasil, os meus cunhados e cunhadas e os netos todos dos meus sogros que, ao todo, são nove.
Beatriz Meu Deus, tanta gente! Deve ter sido um pandemónio com essa malta toda.
Antónia Não, nem por isso. Estava tudo muito bem organizado. Como estava calor, mandámos os mais novos para a piscina e pusemos a gente mais velha a jogar xadrez. Nós, as mulheres, estávamos encarregadas de todos os preparativos, enquanto os maridos bebiam e discutiam os últimos acontecimentos.
Beatriz Quantos anos fez o seu sogro?
Antónia Fez sessenta e cinco anos.
Beatriz Não parece, está muito bem conservado. Quando o vir, dê-lhe

os meus sinceros parabéns. Tem graça que a minha enteada também fez anos no dia vinte e oito. Fez dezoito anos. Mas com essa não tivemos problema. Ela foi para a discoteca com os amigos e nós só pagámos a conta. Voltando ao assunto da sua festa, que comeram?

Antónia Bem, para o almoço tivemos saladas, ovos, queijo, camarões, azeitonas e fruta – muitas uvas e melões e também melancia. Depois da sesta lanchámos: chá, torradas, biscoitos feitos em casa e o bolo dos anos com as velas. E por volta das oito jantámos. Era leitão assado no espeto – no jardim, é claro – ervilhas batatas e outros legumes. Para sobremesa tivemos uma grande variedade de pudins. O vinho era do melhor, das adegas do meu cunhado e, naturalmente, não faltava o champagne.

Please repeat the following expressions:

dia dos anos birthday
uma grande festa a great party
ao todo in all
tanta gente so many people
deve ter sido it must have been
com essa malta toda with all that crowd (*colloquial*)
nem por isso not really, not too bad
quantos anos fez . . . how old was . . .
não parece he does not look it, he does not appear . . .
bem conservado well preserved
quando o vir when you see him
parabéns happy birthday (*also* congratulations)
tem graça how funny, it is funny, what a coincidence
mas com essa with that one, with her
voltando ao assunto coming back to the subject
e por volta das oito and around eight o'clock
era do melhor it was of the best
não faltava we were not short of, there was no lack of

Other vocabulary:

sogro/sogra father-in-law/mother-in-law
praticamente practically
toda a família the whole family
sobrinhos/sobrinhas nephews/nieces
cunhados/cunhadas brothers-in-law/sisters-in-law
netos grandchildren
pandemónio pandemonium (*in Brazil:* **pandemônio**)
organizado organized (*the past participle of verb* **organizar**)
mandámos *past tense of verb* **mandar** to send, to order command
os mais novos the younger ones

pusemos *past tense of verb* **pôr** to put to set (*irregular*)
mais velha older
xadrez chess
estávamos encarregadas we were in charge
enquanto while
os maridos the husbands
discutir to discuss
últimos acontecimentos the latest events
fazer to make, to do
Quantos anos fez? How old were you, was he/she?
dê-lhe give him (*imperative of* **dar**)
enteada stepdaughter
tivemos past tense of verb **ter**
foi went/was
pagar to pay
ovos eggs
queijo cheese
camarões prawns (*also* shrimps)
azeitonas olives
uvas grapes
melões melons
melancia water melon
sesta nap (afternoon nap)
chá tea
torradas toast
biscoitos biscuits
feitos em casa made at home (*verb* **fazer**)
velas candles
leitão suckling pig
assado roasted
espeto spit
jardim garden
é claro of course, naturally
ervilhas peas
batatas potatoes
outros others
legumes vegetables
sobremesa dessert
variedade variety
pudins puddings (*sing.* **pudim**)
vinho wine
adegas wine cellars

Seventh lesson/sétima lição

28 ou ... ou either ... or, **nem ... nem** neither ... nor

Quem manda aqui, sou eu ou você? Who is in charge here, (*literally* who gives orders) is it me or you?

Nem eu nem a minha mulher nem os meus filhos gostamos de ar condicionado. Neither I nor my wife nor my children like air conditioning.

From these sentences the student should note two things: one is that the subject pronoun **eu** comes first when there are other subject pronouns (**Eu e a minha mulher** instead of the English 'My wife and I'); and the other is that in Portuguese you may repeat the word **nem** 'neither, nor' as many times as necessary.

nem and **nem mesmo** translate 'not even'. For example:

Nem quero sonhar uma coisa dessas. I don't even want to think of (*literally* dream of) such a thing.
Nem mesmo se o senhor me pagasse. Not even if you paid me.

Nem is sometimes used in place of **não**. For example:

Nem me diga ... You don't say ... Don't tell me
Nem por isso. Not really.

29 Other negatives

nada nothing
nunca never
nunca mais never again
ninguém no-one
nenhum (*m*), **nenhuma** (*f*), **nenhuns** (*m pl*), **nenhumas** (*f pl*) none, any

Não conheço ninguém aqui. I don't know anyone here.
Ele não tem nenhuma ideia. He hasn't any idea.
Nunca mais compro sapatos de salto alto. Never again will I buy high-heeled shoes.
Eles não têm nada. They have nothing.
Nunca o vi na minha vida. I have never seen him in my life.

Note the use of double negatives in Portuguese.

Exercise 21

1 Você quer tomar chá ou café?
2 Nem quero chá nem café. Prefiro um sumo de laranja.
3 Ou vou ao cinema ou fico em casa, a ver televisão, ainda não tenho a certeza.
4 Nunca vi uma exposição tão bem organizada.
5 Ele não tem escrúpulos nenhuns.
6 Nunca mais compro aparelhos eléctricos em segunda mão.
7 Você não tem nada a ver com isso.
8 Aqui ninguém fala Inglês.
9 Eu não sei nada.
10 Não fomos a lado nenhum.

Vocabulary:

café coffee
sumo de laranja orange juice (*in Brazil:* **suco de laranja**)
ficar to stay, remain
ainda yet, still
não tenho a certeza I am not sure (*in Brazil:* **não estou certo/a**)
exposição exhibition
escrúpulos scruples
aparelhos eléctricos electrical appliances
segunda mão second hand
não ter nada a ver com . . . to have nothing to do with
sei I know (*present tense of* **saber**)
fomos *past definite of* **ir** we went
lado nenhum nowhere, anywhere

30 Other indefinite adjectives and pronouns, variable and invariable

Plurals and genders are given in brackets when applicable.

certo, certa; certos, certas certain
outro, outra; outros, outras other
pouco, pouca little; **poucos, poucas** few
todo, toda; todos, todas every, all
algum, alguma; alguns, algumas some (*also* 'any' *used in questions*)
um, uma; uns, umas one, some (*often used in place of* **algum -a -as**)
tal, tais such
qualquer, quaisquer any (*of a choice – used in affirmative, negative or interrogative sentences*)
ambos, ambas both

alguém somebody ('anybody' *when used in questions*)
cada each
tudo everything
tanto, tanta so much; **tantos, tantas** so many

31 Comparison of adjectives and adverbs

The comparative

The comparative is usually formed by **mais** (more) or **menos** (less) plus the adjective, plus **do que** (or merely **que**):

Ela é mais bonita do que a irmã. She is prettier than her sister, *or*
Ela é mais bonita que a irmã.
Ela tem menos dinheiro do que eu. She has less money than I.

tão . . . como as . . . as
Ela é tão rica como eu. She is as rich as I.

tanto|-a, tantos|-as . . . como as much/many . . . as
Tem tanto dinheiro como eu. She has as much money as I.

In Brazil, for 'as . . . as', say **tão . . . quanto** (or **tanto . . . quanto,** which is also occasionally used in Portugal).

The superlative

The superlative is formed by putting the articles **o, a, os, as,** before **mais, menos** 'more', 'less'. Thus they become 'the most', 'the least'. For example:

Ela é a mais bonita. She is the prettiest.

The superlative 'very' can be rendered by **muito,** and 'extremely' by adding **-íssimo** to the adjective after dropping the final vowel. For example:

Ela é muito bonita. She is very pretty.

lindo beautiful *becomes* **lindíssimo** extremely beautiful
barato cheap *becomes* **baratíssimo** extremely cheap

Some irregular superlatives:

fácil easy *becomes* **facílimo**
rico rich *becomes* **riquíssimo**
feliz happy *becomes* **felicíssimo**
amável kind *becomes* **amabilíssimo**
pobre poor *becomes* **paupérrimo**

Irregular comparatives of adjectives and adverbs

bom, boa good **}** **bem** well	**melhor** better	**o melhor** the best	**óptimo** super
mau, má bad **}** **mal** badly, ill	**pior** worse	**o pior** the worst	**péssimo** extremely bad
grande large, big *etc:*	**maior** larger	**o maior** the largest	**máximo** massive
pequeno small, little:	**mais pequeno** *or* **menor**	**o mais pequeno** *or* **o menor**	**mínimo**
alto tall, high, loud:	**mais alto** *or* **superior**	**o mais alto**	**supremo**
baixo low, short:	**mais baixo** *or* **inferior**	**o mais baixo**	**ínfimo**

Ele é a autoridade suprema. He is the highest authority.
O tempo está péssimo. The weather is awful.
Uma óptima ideia. A super idea.

Adverbs ending in English in -*ly* are generally formed in Portuguese by adding -**mente** to the feminine singular of the adjective. For example:

raro *becomes* **raramente** rarely
absoluto *becomes* **absolutamente** absolutely
fácil *becomes* **facilmente** easily

When two or more adverbs of this type come together, -**mente** is added to the last one only. For example:

Ele falou clara e vagarosamente. He spoke clearly and slowly.

Exercise 22

Translate the following:
1 Does anyone speak English here?
2 Did you (*o senhor*) ask me for a spoon or a knife?
3 Neither. I asked you for a fork.
4 He has some hope.
5 Each to his own taste.
6 Everything is very expensive.
7 Have you any (any of a choice) English magazines?
8 They are both writers.
9 The dinner was awful.
10 My aunt is extremely ill.

11 He is the richest man in the world.
12 I have good news for you.
13 She is as happy as I am.
14 Camoēs was the greatest Portuguese poet.

Vocabulary:

pedir to ask for
colher spoon (*f*)
faca (*f*) knife
nem uma nem outra neither (one nor the other)
garfo (*m*) fork
esperança hope
cada qual each (one)
gosto taste
caro expensive
revistas magazines
escritores writers
do mundo in the world
notícias news
para si for you (*in Brazil:* **para você**)

32 The future and conditional tenses (I will, I would)

These tenses are very easily formed and conjugated. With only three exceptions, the appropriate endings are added to the infinitive of all verbs whether regular or irregular, as shown in the following tables.

Future tense

	falar (to speak) (*regular*)	**ter** (to have) (*irregular*)	**ir** (to go) (*irregular*)
eu	falar**ei**	ter**ei**	ir**ei**
tu	falar**ás**	ter**ás**	ir**ás**
você	falar**á**	ter**á**	ir**á**
ele, ela	falar**á**	ter**á**	ir**á**
nós	falar**emos**	ter**emos**	ir**emos**
vocês	falar**ão**	ter**ão**	ir**ão**
eles, elas	falar**ão**	ter**ão**	ir**ão**

Conditional tense

eu	falaria	teria	iria
tu	falarias	terias	irias
você	falaria	teria	iria
ele, ela	falaria	teria	iria
nós	falaríamos	teríamos	iríamos
vocês	falariam	teriam	iriam
eles, elas	falariam	teriam	iriam

The exceptions: **dizer** to say, **fazer** to make, to do, **trazer** to bring

The future and conditional endings for these verbs are exactly the same as those shown in bold in the tables above. The only difference is that the infinitive to which the endings are added is modified as follows:

dizer *becomes* **dir**ei, -ás, -á, -emos, -ão (*future*)
diria, -ias, -ia, -íamos, -iam (*(conditional)*

fazer *becomes* **far**ei, -ás, -á, -emos, -ão (*future*)
faria, -ias, -ia, -íamos, -iam (*conditional*)

trazer *becomes* **trar**ei, -ás, -á, -emos, -ão (*future*)
traria, -ias, -ia, -íamos, -iam (*conditional*)

Pronominal future and conditional

When the future and conditional tenses are followed by an object pronoun, the pronoun is inserted between the stem – i.e. the infinitive – and the ending. For example:

Dar-lhe-ei . . . I will give him . . . (*not* Darei-lhe . . .)
Eu far-lho-ia. I would do it for you.
Eles falar-me-ão. They will speak to me.

Apart from the change described above and illustrated by the preceding examples, the rules governing formation and position of pronouns apply to the future and conditional tenses in exactly the same way as explained in lesson 6.

1 The pronouns precede the verb in negative and interrogative sentences, and after certain adverbs, prepositions and conjunctions. For example:

Eles não me falarão. They will not speak to me.

2 The *r* of the infinitive is dropped before 3rd person pronouns and an accent or circumflex is placed over the remaining vowel to indicate that it retains its full sound value, as if the *r* were still present. For example:

Fá-lo-ei. I will do it.
Eles comê-lo-ão. They will eat it.

Other ways of expressing the future
(see also section 10, page 24)

1 The present tense

In Portuguese, especially in conversation, it is much more common than in English to use the present tense to express a future intention or action. For example:

Saio amanhã, I'll go out tomorrow. (I'm going out tomorrow.)

2 Use of **ir** + infinitive

Just as in English, it is possible and common in Portuguese to use the present tense of **ir** (to go) with an infinitive to express future intention. For example:

Vou sair amanhã. I'm going to go out tomorrow.

3 Use of **haver de** + infinitive.

This is another method of expressing a strong intention to perform a future action and it has, therefore, the effect of the future tense. For example:

Você há-de aprender português. You will learn Portuguese.

For the full conjugation of **haver** in the present tense, see lesson 1, sections 4 and 6.

Idiomatic uses of the future and conditional tenses

1 The future and conditional tenses can be used to express the idea of 'approximately'. In a situation pertaining to the present, the future tense is used, and in a situation pertaining to the past, the conditional is used. For example:

O nosso professor terá uns cinquenta anos. Our teacher is about fifty years old.
Seriam cinco horas quando ele entrou. He came in at about 5 o'clock.

2 It is possible to use the future and conditional tenses to convey uncertainty in situations where in English it would be natural to use the expression 'to wonder whether . . .'. For example:

Será esta a rua que buscamos*? I wonder whether this is the street we are looking for? (* Brazilian usage. In Portugal say **procuramos.**)
Estaria ele culpado? I wonder whether he was guilty?

Note that as in the preceding examples, the future tense is used to refer to present circumstances and the conditional to refer to past events.

Use of the imperfect to replace the conditional

The imperfect tense can be used as a substitute for the conditional when the meaning is 'I would' etc. For example:

Gostava de ir ao Brasil = Gostaria de ir ao Brasil. I would like to go to Brazil.

However, the imperfect cannot be used to replace the conditional when the conditional is used in one of the idiomatic senses described above. (See also section 27, page 63).

Exercise 23

Translate the following:
1 When will you write to him?
2 He has to work hard.
3 We shall not take it.
4 I shall begin my story.
5 Who will win?
6 We shall arrive (in the) next month.
7 Was it (Would it be) true?
8 Eu diria que ele está a mentir.
9 Não me esquecerei de ti.
10 Faria tudo por ela.
11 Eles dar-lhe-ão a minha nova morada.
12 Hei-de ir ao Japão.
13 Tenho de ir ao dentista.
14 Será muito caro?

Vocabulary:

escrever to write
muito hard
começar to begin
ganhar to win
chegar to arrive
verdade true
mentir to lie
nova new
esquecer-se to forget
Japão Japan
dentista dentist
caro expensive

CONVERSATION

Um lugar ao sol/a place in the sun

António Ando à procura de casa no Algarve, mas não encontro nada em conta. Devia ter comprado há anos quando o Algarve ainda não era tão conhecido no estrangeiro.

Carlos Você já pôs um anúncio no jornal?

António Sim já pus mas não recebi nenhuma resposta de interesse; é sempre a mesma história: as casas de que gosto são caras demais, e aquelas que são baratas precisam de muitas obras e são muito longe do mar. Quanto aos apartamentos, fazem-me lembrar caixas de fósforos.

Carlos Você é muito exigente. Já sabe se quer coisa boa tem de pagar, especialmente num sítio como o Algarve.

António Sim, já sei; no entanto continuarei a tentar. Ainda tenho esperanças de arranjar uma casinha de pescadores à beira-mar com um pequeno jardim, com três ou quatro quartos, sala, casa de jantar, cozinha e casa de banho com chuveiro, e que custe entre as vinte e vinte e cinco mil libras.

Carlos É tudo? Quando encontrar essa raridade, veja lá se arranja duas; eu até lhe pagaria uma comissão com muito prazer.

Learn the following expressions:

Ando à procura . . . I am looking for . . . (*In Portuguese there are a number of nouns taken from verbs – in this case from* **procurar** *to look for*)
em conta reasonably priced
Devia ter comprado há anos. I should have bought (it) years ago.
tão conhecido so well-known
caras demais too dear (*alternative:* **demasiado caras**)
quanto a . . . as to . . . (as for)
fazem-me lembrar . . . they remind me of . . . (*literally* they make me remember . . .)
muito exigente very demanding, hard to please
Já sabe. You know.
Já sei. I know. (I am well aware.)
no entanto nevertheless
Ainda tenho esperanças. I still have hopes.
casinha de pescadores a little fishermen's cottage (*The diminutive suffixes* **-inho/a, -zinho/a, -zito/a, -ito/a** *are often used in Portuguese, denoting smallness, affection or pity.*)
e que custe . . . and which costs . . . (*The use of the subjunctive is explained in lesson 9*)
É tudo? Is that all?

Veja lá se arranja duas. See if you find (get) two. (**lá** *meaning 'there' is often used in an abstract sense in colloquial speech, much as the English say 'Look here.'*)

E eu até lhe pagaria. I would even pay you. (**até** *meaning 'until', also means 'even' in this context.*)

Other vocabulary:

encontrar to find, to meet
no estrangeiro abroad
estrangeiro/a foreigner
Já pôs . . ? Have you put . .?
pôr (*irregular*) to put
anúncio advertisement
jornal newspaper
resposta reply, answer
história story, history
baratas cheap.
obra repairs (to house), construction, literary work, opus
caixa de fósforos a box of matches
se if, whether
querer to want
coisa boa a good thing
sítio place
tentar to try, to attempt
beira-mar by the sea
quartos bedrooms
sala (de visitas) sitting-room
casa de jantar dining-room
cozinha kitchen
chuveiro shower
comissão commission

Eighth lesson/oitava lição

33 The past participle

The regular past participle is formed by changing the endings of the infinitive (**-ar**, **-er** and **-ir**) for **-ado**, **-ido** and **-ido** respectively. The forms are therefore as follows:

infinitive	*past participle*	
dar	**dado**	(given)
vender	**vendido**	(sold)
mentir	**mentido**	(lied)

Some past participles are irregular; these are listed below:

infinitive	*past participle*
pôr to put	**posto**
abrir to open	**aberto**
fazer to do, to make	**feito**
escrever to write	**escrito**
dizer to say, to tell	**dito**
vir to come	**vindo**
ver to see	**visto**
pagar to pay	**pago**
gastar to spend	**gasto**
ganhar to earn, to win, to gain	**ganho**

Some verbs have two past participles: a regular form which remains invariable and is used with the auxiliary verb **ter** to form compound tenses, and an irregular form which can be used as an adjective with the auxiliary verbs **ser** and **estar**. When used as an adjective, the participle agrees with the noun it qualifies in number and gender. The most important irregular forms are given below:

infinitive	*regular*	*irregular*
romper to tear	**rompido**	**roto**
prender to arrest	**prendido**	**preso**
aceitar to accept	**aceitado**	**aceito, aceite**
enxugar to dry	**enxugado**	**enxuto**
limpar to clean	**limpado**	**limpo**
acender to light	**acendido**	**aceso**

matar to kill	matado	morto
expulsar to expel	expulsado	expulso
morrer to die	morrido	morto
suspender to suspend	suspendido	suspenso

A roupa está quáse enxuta. The clothes are nearly dry.
Eu já tinha enxugado a louça. I had already dried the dishes.
A luz está acesa. The light is on.
Ele já tinha acendido o fogão. He had already lit the fire.

34 The perfect/pluperfect tenses

These compound tenses are formed, as in English, with the auxiliary **ter** (to have) and the past participle of the main verb. The perfect uses the verb **ter** in the present indicative and expresses an action carried from the past up to the present, or almost up to the present. For example:

Tenho falado. I have been speaking.

The perfect must not be confused with the past definite ('I have spoken') which expresses an action completed in the past. (You will remember that the Portuguese past definite is not a compound tense – it is simply **falei** 'I spoke'.)

The pluperfect has the verb **ter** in the imperfect and indicates an action in the past prior to another past action, the same as in English:

Tinha falado. I had spoken.

Here are a few examples showing all four past tenses.

Ontem falei com a tua irmã. Yesterday I spoke to your sister. (*past definite*)
Falava com a tua mãe. I was speaking to your mother. (*imperfect*)
Ultimamente tenho falado muito francês. I have been speaking a lot of French lately. (*perfect*)
Já tinha falado com o meu patrão antes de você me pedir para o fazer. I had already spoken to my boss before you asked me to do it. (*pluperfect*)

There is a fifth tense, also called the pluperfect, which is not a compound tense and is therefore in Portuguese **mais que perfeito simples** while the pluperfect shown above is called **mais que perfeito composto**. The simple pluperfect is seldom used in colloquial speech. (See the Appendix, p.142.)

35 Reflexive verbs

A reflexive verb is one in which the object of the verb is the same person or thing as the subject, where the action reflects back on the subject. Reflexive verbs are much more common in Portuguese than in English. They are formed by combining the reflexive pronouns **me, te, se** etc, with the appropriate part of the verb. The pronoun comes before or after the verb according to the rules explained in section 25, page 57. Although the reflexive pronoun can be translated as 'myself', 'yourself', etc, it is not usually natural in English to translate it at all.

Some reflexive verbs:

levantar-se to get up
lembrar-se de to remember
esquecer-se de to forget
sentar-se to sit down
lavar-se to wash oneself, to have a wash
barbear-se to shave oneself
deitar-se to go to bed, to lie down
vestir-se to get dressed
despir-se to get undressed
pentear-se to comb one's hair
banhar-se to bathe
divertir-se to enjoy oneself
habituar-se a to get used to
sentir-se to feel
decidir-se a to decide to

Não me lembrava da tua morada. I could not remember your address.
Eles vão-se lavar. They are going to get washed.
Divertimo-nos muito na sua festa. We enjoyed ourselves very much at your party.
Por favor sente-se. Please sit down.
Avie-se. *or* **Despache-se.** Hurry up.
Você enganou-se. You made a mistake.
Sirva-se. Help yourself.

Use of ***mesmo*** *and* ***próprio*** *to translate 'myself', 'yourself', etc*

In English, the forms 'myself', 'yourself', etc, are also used to give emphasis to the subject. This is expressed in Portuguese *not* by the reflexive pronoun but by the use of the adjectives **mesmo** and **próprio**, which agree with the subject in number and gender:

Eu própria lhe contei a história. I myself told him the story.
Nós mesmos não queríamos ir. We ourselves did not want to go.
Ele mesmo veio falar comigo. He came himself to speak to me.

36 The reciprocal form

Reciprocal actions, although different from reflexive verbs, require the use of the reflexive pronoun. For example:

Nós encontrámo-nos por acaso. We met by chance.
Eles amam-se. They love each other.
Elas não se conhecem. They don't know each other.
Nunca nos vimos. We have never seen each other.

To avoid ambiguity between the reflexive and reciprocal forms, the phrase **um ao outro** (one another) is sometimes added to make it clear that the verb is reciprocal. This is especially important in cases where the verb is naturally reflexive. The phrase **um ao outro** varies according to the number and gender of the subjects involved:

um ao outro (two *m sing.* subjects)
uma à outra (two *f sing.* subjects)
uns aos outros more than two *m pl* or mixed *m & f pl* subjects)
umas às outras (more than two *f pl* subjects)

and so on.

Consider the following example:

Eles enganam-se *would normally mean* They are making a mistake.
But it could mean They are deceiving each other.

To make the latter meaning absolutely clear, it is necessary to add the appropriate form of **um ao outro**. For example:

A minha irmã e o cunhado enganam-se um ao outro. My sister and brother-in-law deceive each other.

37 The passive voice and 'se' as impersonal subject pronoun

The passive voice is formed with the verb **ser** and the past participle, which must agree in number and gender with the subject. It is not as much used as the English passive voice, which is often translated by the Portuguese active voice plus the indeterminate pronoun **se**, that is, reflexively – **se** forms an impersonal subject pronoun. For example:

Aqui fala-se português. Portuguese is spoken here.
Disseram-me que . . . I was told that . . . (*literally* They told me that . . .)
Diz-se que ela é muito rica. It is said that she is very rich. *or* –
Dizem que ela é muito rica. It is said that she is very rich. (*literally* They say that she is very rich.)

Vê-se muita gente nas ruas no Natal. Many people are seen in the streets at Christmas.

Aqui vendem-se jornais. Newspapers are sold here.

The passive voice is followed by the preposition **por** ('by'), combined with the articles in the usual way:

A carta foi escrita pela irmã. The letter was written by (his/her) sister.
Ela é amada por todos. She is loved by everybody.

Exercise 24

Translate the following:
1 Ela já tinha estudado português quando era criança.
2 Este ano tem havido muitos desastres de avião.
3 A mulher já estava morta quando o médico chegou.
4 As mesas já estavam postas mas os convidados ainda não tinham chegado.
5 Eu nunca tinha visto tanta gente na minha vida.
6 Ela foi expulsa da escola.
7 Diz-se que a firma Agiota & Co. vai falir.
8 Não se deve enganar os outros.
9 Elas ainda não se tinham lavado.
10 Tem feito muito mau tempo.

Vocabulary:

criança child
desastres accidents, disasters
convidados guests
tanta gente so many people
vida life
falir to fold up, to go bankrupt
enganar to cheat
lavar-se to have a wash (*literally* to wash oneself)
fazer bom/mau tempo to have good/bad weather

38 Impersonal verbs

There are a number of verbs which are used in the 3rd person singular only. The most common of these are **há** (there is, there are) and expressions describing the weather (such as **chove** it is raining, **neva** it is snowing). Other examples are:

Faz calor.   It is hot.
Faz frio.   It is cold.

Faz sol.	It is sunny.
Faz vento.	It is windy.

Exercise 25

Translate the following:
1 Eles sentiam-se desanimados.
2 Levantei-me muito cedo.
3 Ele nunca se lembra dos meus anos.
4 Ela vestiu-se à pressa.
5 Ele cheira mal porque nunca se lava.
6 Como se diz 'table' em português?
7 Eles olharam-se um ao outro.
8 Sirva-se enquanto a comida está quente.
9 Não nos conhecemos
10 Eu queixei-me à polícia.
11 Vá-se embora.
12 Faz sol
13 Esqueci-me dele.
14 Aqui vendem-se jornais ingleses.

Vocabulary:

desanimados disappointed
cedo early
meus anos my birthday
pressa hurry
cheirar to smell
olhar to look at
comida food
queixar-se to complain
ir-se embora to go away, to leave

Exercise 26

Translate the following:
1 I remember him.
2 I was not feeling well.
3 We complained about the food.
4 It has been raining a lot this year.
5 I had already mailed the letter.
6 A lot of wine is drunk in Portugal but the Portuguese never get drunk.
7 The window was open.
8 The lottery was won by a poor woman.

9 My skirt was torn.
10 They were all arrested.
11 They looked at each other.
12 I have not travelled (been travelling) this year.
13 One hears a lot of British music in Portugal.
14 I do not want to help myself.
15 We saw each other by chance.
16 Newspapers are sold here.

Vocabulary:

pôr a carta no correio to mail a letter
embriagar-se to get drunk
lotaria lottery
saia skirt
viajar to travel
rasgar to tear
ganhar to win
prender to arrest

CONVERSATION

No restaurante/at the restaurant

o senhor Carvalho	Boa noite, tem uma mesa livre?
o criado de mesa	O senhor não reservou?
o senhor Carvalho	Não, não tive tempo, foi uma coisa resolvida à última hora.
o criado	Vou ver. Quantas pessoas são?
o senhor Carvalho	Quatro. Preferia uma mesa ao pé da janela, pois está muito calor.
o criado	Lamento muito mas as mesas ao pé das janelas estão todas reservadas. Esta aqui agrada-lhe?
o senhor Carvalho	Que remédio! Traga-nos a ementa por favor e a lista dos vinhos. O que nos recomenda?
o criado	Recomendo-lhes o prato do dia que é especialidade cá da casa 'bacalhau de cebolada', ou então 'porco com ameijoas à alentejana' que é um grande petisco português.
o senhor Carvalho	Pois bem, traga esse para mim, 'bacalhau de cebolada' para a minha filha, um bife 'à transmontana' para a minha mulher, e para o meu amigo 'frango na púcara'.
o criado	Que legumes?
o senhor Carvalho	Ervilhas e batatas fritas para dois, puré de batata e feijão verde para outro e arroz e salada de alface e pepino para mim.

o criado	E para beber, o que desejam?
o senhor Carvalho	Vinho da casa. Uma garrafa de tinto e uma de branco. Traga também dois cafezinhos – um simples e um com leite para terminar o jantar pois não queremos sobremesa. Queria também que me trouxesse a conta porque estamos com muita pressa; vamos a um concerto e não podemos chegar atrasados.

No hotel/at the hotel

o senhor Jones	Boa tarde. Chamo-me Jones. Escrevi a marcar um quarto de casal e um quarto para pessoa só.
a recepcionista	Um momento se faz favor. Ora, aqui está . . . Senhor Jones, dois quartos para o dia dezoito. Há aqui um problema; aparentemente o meu colega deu estes quartos a outras pessoas porque pensava que os senhores não viessem. Nós só reservamos os quartos até ao meio-dia. Como devem compreender esta é a época dos turistas e há falta de acomodação.
o senhor Jones	Que falta de consideração! Não sabe que hoje em dia os aviões chegam e partem quando lhes apetecem? Não é nossa culpa se chegamos atrasados. Nós já lhe tínhamos escrito a fazer esta marcação e os senhores responderam a confirmá-la. Isto não se pode admitir. Estamos cansados e aborrecidos e agora não temos quartos. Eu daqui não saio até que me arranjem acomodação.
a recepcionista	Peço imensa desculpa por este lapso da nossa parte. Vou ver o que se pode arranjar. (*A recepcionista depois de uns minutos, regressa.*) Estamos com sorte. Falei com o gerente que me disse para lhes dar o apartamento de luxo que está normalmente reservado para certas entidades e ocasiões especiais. Os senhores podem tê-lo pelo mesmo preço que os quartos que tinham reservado, lhes custariam. É claro que só o podemos dar por duas noites. Depois se verá.
o senhor Jones	Não faz mal. Estamos gratos por este gesto amável. A que horas servem o pequeno-almoço?
a recepcionista	Das sete às nove e meia. Desejam meia-pensão ou pensão completa?
o senhor Jones	Preferimos pensão completa. E gostaríamos que nos acordassem às oito em ponto com três chávenas de chá à Inglesa.

a recepcionista Muito bem; Aqui está a vossa chave. O empregado vai
levar-vos as malas.

Vocabulary:

AT THE RESTAURANT
Foi uma coisa resolvida à última hora. It was a last minute thing.
ao pé da near, close to
Esta aqui agrada-lhe? Will this one do?
bacalhau de cebolada cod in onions (**bacalhau**, salted cod, is the national dish).
à transmontana cooked in the fashion of Trás-os-Montes, a northern province of Portugal
porco com ameijoas à alentejana pork with clams in the fashion of Alentejo, a province south of the River Tagus
frango na púcara traditional Portuguese dish, 'chicken in the pot' which is cooked in an earthenware pot with herbs.
legumes vegetables
ervilhas peas
batatas fritas fried potatoes
puré de batata mashed potato
feijão verde green beans
arroz rice
alface lettuce
pepino cucumber
garrafa bottle, *also* carafe
tinto red
branco white
cafezinhos coffees (*diminutive form**)
um café simples a black coffee (*also known as* **uma bica**)
café com leite white coffee (*slang:* **garoto**)
pois as, for, because
sobremesa dessert
a conta the bill

AT THE HOTEL
marcar to book
um quarto de casal a double bedroom
para pessoa só single room
falta de shortage of
Que falta de consideração! What lack of consideration!
quando lhes apetece when they feel like it
hoje em dia nowadays
Não é nossa culpa. It is not our fault.
marcação booking
Isto não se pode admitir. This is unacceptable.
Eu daqui não saio I am not leaving here

até que me arranjem . . . until you find me . . .
peço imensa desculpa I am so very sorry
lapso da nossa parte oversight on our part
o que se pode arranjar what can be done
gerente manager
certas entidades certain personalities (VIPS)
depois se verá we shall see after that
Não faz mal. It does not matter.
gesto amável kind gesture
pequeno-almoço breakfast (*in Brazil:* **café da manhã**)
meia pensão half board
pensão completa full board
acordar to wake someone up
chávenas de chá cups of tea (*In Brazil:* **xícara**. This word is still in use in the Portuguese countryside and in culinary language.)
chave key
levar-vos as malas to take the suitcases for you

*The affectionate temperament of the Portuguese is reflected in their language by the diminutives **-inho, -zinho, -ito, -zito.** These are added to the noun or object, to express affection, commiseration or smallness. Thus you may find **favor** changed to **favorzinho**, and **obrigada** changed to **obrigadinha**.

Ninth lesson/nona lição

39 The present subjunctive

The present subjunctive is not a difficult tense to form and conjugate. If you forget the final -r of the infinitive, you'll see that verbs belonging to the 'a' conjugation end in **e**, whereas those of the second and third conjugations ('e' and 'i') end in **a**. The following table shows the basic principle for changing from the present indicative to the subjunctive.

Regular verbs

	falar (to speak)	**comer** (to eat)	**partir** (to leave)
eu	fal**e**	com**a**	part**a**
tu	fal**es**	com**as**	part**as**
você	fal**e**	com**a**	part**a**
ele, ela	fal**e**	com**a**	part**a**
nós	fal**emos**	com**amos**	part**amos**
vocês	fal**em**	com**am**	part**am**
eles, elas	fal**em**	com**am**	part**am**

Exceptions and irregular verbs

The present subjunctive of irregular verbs is formed from the 1st person singular of the present indicative by removing the letter **o** and adding the endings **-a, -as, -a, -amos, -am**. For example:

faz**er**→faç**o**→faç**a**, faç**as**, faç**a**, faç**amos**, faç**am**

There are seven exceptions to the general rule, as follows:

ser	estar	dar	haver	saber	querer	ir
seja	esteja	dê	haja	saiba	queira	vá
sejas	estejas	dês	hajas	saibas	queiras	vás
seja	esteja	dê	haja	saiba	queira	vá
sejamos	estejamos	dêmos	hajamos	saibamos	queiramos	vamos
sejam	estejam	dêem	hajam	saibam	queiram	vão

See also the table of verbs in the Appendix.

40 Uses of the subjunctive mood

Generally speaking the subjunctive expresses a possibility, something yet to happen, or something contrary to actual fact. It corresponds to 'may', 'should' and 'might' in English.

The subjunctive is used in subordinate clauses:

1 after the verb in the main clause expresses doubt, command, denial, wish, prohibition, permission, hope, request, regret; and verbs of emotion (to be sorry, to be sad, to be happy, to fear)

Main clause	Subordinate clause
Quero	**que você saia.**
I want	you to go out. (*literally* that you should go out)

Duvido que ele venha hoje. I doubt whether he will come today. (*literally* that he may come)
Espero que ela esteja melhor. I hope she is better.
Lamento que não possamos vir. I regret that we are not able to come.
Folgo muito que seja assim. I am so happy that it is so.
Temo que haja uma guerra. I fear there may be a war.
Temos pena que eles não falem português. We are sorry that they don't speak Portuguese.

2 In impersonal sentences

É preciso que vocês estudem muito. It is necessary for you to study hard. (You must study hard.) 'É preciso' corresponds to the French 'il faut'.
É provável que eu vá ao Japão. It is probable that I will go to Japan.

3 After verbs in the negative which express an opinion or thought

Não acho que ele seja malcriado. I don't think he is ill-mannered.
Não creio que o governo vá mudar. I don't believe the government is going to change.

Note: the affirmative is rendered in the indicative:
Creio que o governo vai mudar. I believe the government is going to change.

4 After indefinite antecedents (i.e. when the subject is general or not defined)

Há aqui alguém que fale Inglês? Is there anyone here who speaks English?
Procuro uma casa que seja barata. I am looking for a house that is cheap.

Compare: **Procuro a casa que está anunciada no jornal.** I am looking for the house that is advertised in the paper.
Here the subject is specifically identified and the indicative should be used.

5 After **talvez, tomara** and **oxalá** (see lesson 5, conversation vocabulary)

Talvez seja verdade. Maybe it is true.
Oxalá amanhã não chova. I hope it does not rain tomorrow.
Tomara que ele não venha. I hope/wish he doesn't come.

Note that **tomara** is used in northern Portugal and Brazil, while **oxalá** (due to its Arabic derivation) is more frequently heard in Lisbon and the south.

6 After the following conjunctions (adverbial clauses)

a não ser que unless
antes que before
até que until
ainda que although, though
embora though, although
mesmo que even if
se bem que even though, although
contanto que provided that
para que so that, in order that
sem que without

Janto consigo contanto que você pague a conta. I shall dine with you provided you pay the bill.
Vamos agora sair antes que chova. We are going to leave now before it rains.

Exercise 27

Translate the following:
1 É preciso que eles estudem muito.
2 Oxalá eles não venham tarde.
3 Talvez eu saia amanhã.
4 Quero que você faça isso imediatamente.
5 Diga-lhe que não entre até que eu o chame.
6 Espero que a sua mulher esteja melhor.
7 Não acho que ele seja um bom jogador de futebol.
8 Queremos um homem que tenha a coragem das suas convicções.
9 Quer queira quer não queira, tenho de assistir à reunião amanhã.
10 Tell him not to go to the meeting.
11 Although I don't speak Portuguese very well, I understand everything.
12 Do you want me to bring you the wine list?
13 It is better for me to go now.
14 I don't think there are any newspapers today.
15 They are sorry you cannot come tonight.
16 Please don't make any noise.

Note: please remember the polite form of command (imperative) is in fact a subjunctive.

Vocabulary:
até until
jogador player
quer queira quer não queira whether I like it or not
reunião meeting
lista dos vinhos wine list
barulho noise, commotion

41 The imperfect subjunctive

The imperfect subjunctive of regular verbs is formed by removing the final letter **r** from the infinitive and adding the endings shown in the table below.

	falar (to speak)	**comer** (to eat)	**partir** (to leave)
eu	falasse	comesse	partisse
tu	falasses	comesses	partisses
você	falasse	comesse	partisse
ele, ela	falasse	comesse	partisse
nós	falássemos	comêssemos	partíssemos
vocês	falassem	comessem	partissem
eles, elas	falassem	comessem	partissem

The imperfect subjunctive of irregular verbs is formed by removing the ending **-mos** from the 1st person plural of the past definite tense (see section 23, page 51), and adding the endings shown in bold in the table above. For example:

fazer→fize|**mos** (*past definite*)→fize**sse**, fize**sses**, fize**ssemos**, fize**ssem**

There are no exceptions to this rule. The imperfect subjunctive of some common irregular verbs is given below.

dar→de|mos→desse, desses, déssemos, dessem
haver→houve|mos→houvesse, houvesses, houvéssemos, houvessem
ser⎫
ir ⎭→fo|mos→fosse, fosses, fôssemos, fossem
ter→tive|mos→tivesse, tivesses, tivéssemos, tivessem
vir→vie|mos→viesse, viesses, viéssemos, viessem
ver→vi|mos→visse, visses, víssemos, vissem
estar→estive|mos→estivesse, estivesses, estivéssemos, estivessem
dizer→disse|mos→dissesse, dissesses, disséssemos, dissessem

Use of the imperfect subjunctive

The imperfect subjunctive is used in the same circumstances as the present subjunctive when the verb in the main clause is in the past tense or conditional tense. For example:

Queria que ele arranjasse um emprego melhor. I wanted him to get a better job.

Disse-lhe que não se fosse embora. I told him not to go away.

Ele pediu-me que lhe dissesse que não podia vir. He asked me to tell you that he could not come.

42 The future subjunctive

The future subjunctive of the regular verbs is formed as follows:

	falar (to speak)	**comer** (to eat)	**partir** (to leave)
eu	falar	comer	partir
tu	falares	comeres	partires
você	falar	comer	partir
ele, ela	falar	comer	partir
nós	falarmos	comermos	partirmos
vocês	falarem	comerem	partirem
eles, elas	falarem	comerem	partirem

The future subjunctive of irregular verbs is formed by removing the ending -mos from the 1st person plural of the past definite tense and adding the endings shown in bold in the table above. For example:

fazer→fize|mos→fizer, fizeres, fizermos, fizerem

Use of the future subjunctive

The future subjunctive is used when referring to actions or events, the performance or fulfilment of which is either uncertain or dependent on the completion of another action or event which has not taken place at the time of speaking. It is introduced most commonly by the following words:

quando when, whenever
se if
enquanto que while
assim que as soon as

logo que as soon as
como as
conforme according to
o que whatever
quem whoever
aquele, aquela que whoever
aqueles, aquelas que those who

The following example makes the use of this tense easier to appreciate.

Quando nós formos a Portugal, escrever-te-emos. When we go to Portugal, we will write to you. (*Both actions will take place in the future and one is dependent on the successful completion of the other.*)

Set expressions using present and future subjunctive

There are a number of set formulae in Portuguese which follow the pattern of *present + future subjunctive*. The most common of these are listed below.

Aconteça o que acontecer . . . Whatever happens . . .
Haja o que houver . . . Whatever there may be . . .
Seja quem for . . . Whoever it may be . . . Whoever you may be . . . (*formal*)
Diga o que quiser . . . Say what you like . . .
Seja onde for . . . Wherever it may be . . .
Faça como quiser . . . Do as you please . . .

Many other permutations are possible, using this model structure.

43 Perfect and pluperfect subjunctive

These compound tenses are formed quite easily by combining the present and imperfect subjunctive of the auxiliary **ter** with the past participle as shown in the table below.

	perfect subjunctive	*pluperfect subjunctive*
eu	tenha falado	tivesse falado
tu	tenhas falado	tivesses falado
você	tenha falado	tivesse falado
ele, ela	tenha falado	tivesse falado
nós	tenhamos falado	tivéssemos falado
vocês	tenham falado	tivessem falado
eles, elas	tenham falado	tivessem falado

These compound subjunctive tenses are used in the situations described under *Uses of the subjunctive mood* in section 40, page 90. The following examples illustrate this:

After verbs of emotion
Espero que tenha vindo. I hope he has come.
Esperava que tivesse vindo. I hoped he had come.

After impersonal expressions
É provável que ele tenha ido a Lisboa. It is likely that he has gone to Lisbon.
Era provável que ele tivesse ido a Lisboa. It was likely that he had gone to Lisbon.

After verbs expressing opinion in the negative
Não creio que tenham chegado. I don't think they have arrived.
Não pensei que tivessem chegado. I didn't think they had arrived.

After indefinite antecedents
Há aqui alguém que tenha visto o meu irmão? Is there anyone here who has seen my brother?
Havia lá alguém que tivesse visto o seu irmão? Was there anyone there who had seen your brother?

After talvez, tomara and oxalá
Talvez tenham chegado. Perhaps they have arrived.
Talvez não o tivessem ouvido. Maybe they had not heard him.
Oxalá não tenha falado com os meus pais! I do hope he hasn't spoken to my parents!
Oxalá me tivesses dado ouvidos! If only you had listened to me!

In adverbial clauses
Dar-lhe-ei as mercadorias contanto que tenha pago a conta. I will give you the goods provided that you have paid the bill.
Ter-lhe-ia dado as mercadorias contanto que você tivesse pago a conta. I would have given you the goods provided you had paid the bill.

The pluperfect subjunctive is also used in 'if' clauses referring to hypothetical or impossible situations. This is explained in more detail in the next section.

44 'If' clauses

The word for 'if' in Portuguese is **se**. The sequence of tenses used with **se** is determined according to the following system:

1 Se referring to real facts

These sentences follow the pattern 'If A is true, then B is true.' In such cases, **se** is followed by the indicative mood. For example:

Se ela compra uma propriedade, é porque tem dinheiro. If she buys a property it is because she has the money.
Se o marido chegava atrasado, ela inquietava-se. If her husband arrived late, she used to worry.

In this type of sentence, it should normally be possible to substitute 'when' for 'if' without substantially changing the meaning. This is a useful identification test in 'if' sentences.

2 Se meaning 'whether'

When **se** means 'whether', it is always followed by the indicative mood. For example:

Não sei se ele vem. I do not know whether he is coming.
Ao rei não lhe importava se morriam os súbditos. The king did not care whether his subjects were dying.
Não me disse se eles tinham chegado. He didn't tell me whether they had arrived.

3 Se referring to possible events which have not yet happened

In sentences involving actions or events which are possible but have not been completed or fulfilled at the time of speaking, the future subjunctive is used. For example:

Se te lembrares, traz-me pêssegos de Portugal. If you remember, bring me some peaches from Portugal.
Se formos a Portugal, trar-te-emos pêssegos. If we go to Portugal, we will bring you peaches.

4 Se referring to impossible or hypothetical events

When **se** refers to actions or events which are imaginary or speculative, such as those invented for the sake of argument, the imperfect subjunctive is used. For example:

Se fosse rico, iria dar uma volta ao mundo. If I were rich, I would travel round the world.
Se ela tivesse dinheiro, comprava uma propriedade. If she had money, she would buy a property.

When referring to actions or events in the past which might have happened but did not in fact take place, the pluperfect subjunctive is used. For example:

Se tivéssemos sabido disso, não teríamos dito nada. If we had known that, we would not have said anything.

Exercise 28

Translate the following:

1 Foi pena que ele não pudesse vir.
2 Eu queria que vocês aprendessem português tão depressa quanto possível.
3 Não vi nenhuma casa que me agradasse.
4 Talvez ele tivesse já partido.
5 Se não fosse tão caro comprávamos uma quinta no Algarve.
6 Não queríamos que vocês trouxessem presentes.
7 Não sei se chove.
8 Se chover levo um guarda-chuva.
9 Enquanto os operários não recomeçarem o trabalho não podemos aumentar a produção.
10 Vem a nossa casa quando quiseres.
11 Assim que você arranjar um emprego em Moçambique, diga-me.
12 Faça o que puder.
13 Convidem quem desejarem.
14 Aquele que quiser vir comigo que venha.

Vocabulary:

tão depressa quanto possível as soon as possible
agradar to please
guarda-chuva umbrella
operários workmen, factory workers
aumentar to increase
vem come (*familiar singular imperative*)
faça do
convidar to invite
desejar to wish

Exercise 29

Translate the following:

1 As soon as you (*familiar*) can, please ring me up.
2 If he were not so lazy, he would not have lost that job.
3 It was necessary for them to call the police.
4 I told them to go away.
5 Whatever you say, I don't believe she is dishonest.
6 When I retire, I shall write many books.
7 You may do as you wish.
8 Whatever happens and in spite of the weather, I shall always love England.
9 There was no-one who spoke English.
10 While you (*pl*) are in my house, you are my guests.

11 I was sorry they were not able to come.
12 If you have lost this opportunity, it is because you wanted to.
13 Although they protested many times, the situation remained the same.

Vocabulary:

preguiçoso, mandrião, mandriona (*f*) lazy
ir-se embora to go away
desonesta dishonest
reformar-se, aposentar-se retire
apesar de in spite of
convidados guests
oportunidade opportunity
protestar to complain, to protest
muitas vezes many times
continuou na mesma remained the same

CONVERSATION

Uma avaria de automóvel/a car breakdown

Joaquina	Olá, como estás? Então por cá?
Mafalda	Sim cheguei ontem, às quatro da tarde. Ainda tentei telefonar-te mas o teu telefone estava impedido.
Joaquina	Pois estava. Era o meu marido que estava a fazer um telefonema para a França. Foi por sinal, uma chamada caríssima, porque ele esteve a falar com o sócio francês dele, quáse uma hora.
E tu que me contas? Vieste de barco?
Mafalda	Não, por acaso não. Vim de automóvel pela França e Espanha.
Joaquina	O quê? Vieste sozinha por aí fora?
Mafalda	Não, não; vim com duas amigas.A viagem correu muito bem até chegarmos à vizinhança de Salamanca. De repente o carro deu um solavanco, derrapou para o sentido contrário e parou, felizmente sem nenhum embate. A surpresa foi tão grande e tudo se passou tão rapidamente que nem nos apercebemos do perigo. O susto veio depois do sucedido, por assim dizer. Descobrimos que era um furo no pneu. Infelizmente tinha-me esquecido de trazer as ferramentas.
Joaquina	Mas que disparate que fizeste!
Mafalda	Bem sei, e jurei nunca mais fazê-lo. Enfim lá veio um carro que parou. Calcula tu que o motorista era um médico! Fiquei consternada pois talvez ele estivesse a caminho da casa dum doente. Ele foi muito amável e mudou-nos a roda. Ainda bem que não me tinha esquecido do pneu sobresselente.

Joaquina	Também digo! Foi este o único azar que tiveram?
Mafalda	Não. Assim que passámos a fronteira – onde por sinal os funcionários da alfândega foram muito amáveis – o carro teve outra avaria.
Joaquina	Não me digas! Mas que pouca sorte!
Mafalda	É verdade! Graças a Deus encontrámos um bom mecânico que atendeu à embraiagem, afinou os travões e carregou a bateria. Foi uma despesa com que não contávamos e a falta deste dinheiro faz-nos uma grande diferença.
Joaquina	Mas naturalmente! Faria a qualquer pessoa. Olha, vê lá que já são cinco horas. Ai, meu Deus, como o tempo voa! Tenho que me encontrar com o meu marido às cinco e meia para depois irmos à 'soirée' duma peça que tem tido muito êxito. Telefona-me amanhã para marcarmos o dia que vens a minha casa para jantar. Um dia que estejas disponível. Adeus, até amanhã.

Vocabulary:

avaria breakdown (*applies to anything out of order, like the TV, etc*)
Então por cá? What? You over here?
tentar to try, to attempt
impedido engaged (*telephone*)
por sinal as it happens, as a matter of fact
sócio partner
contar to tell
por acaso actually, as a matter of fact
sozinha alone
por aí fora all that way
correu muito bem went very well
vizinhança neighbourhood, proximity of, outskirts of
de repente suddenly
solavanco jolt
derrapar to skid
contrário opposite
embate collision (*in Brazil:* **descontrole**)
embater to collide with
perigo danger
sucedido event
por assim dizer so to speak
furo no pneu puncture in the tyre
infelizmente unfortunately
ferramentas tools
disparate foolish mistake, silly thing, nonsense
bem sei I know
jurei I swore
fiquei consternada I was dismayed, aghast (I was so embarrassed)

roda wheel
Ainda bem Just as well, so pleased/relieved
pneu sobresselente spare tyre
Também digo! I'll say so! I agree!
o único azar the only piece of bad luck
fronteira frontier
funcionários officers
alfândega Customs
que pouca sorte what bad luck
Graças a Deus thank God
embraiagem clutch
afinar os travões to adjust the brakes (*in Brazil:* **acertar os freios**)
carregar a bateria to charge the battery
despesa expense
com que não contávamos which we did not expect, which we were not counting on
Olha! Oh look!
vê lá imagine
Meu Deus goodness me, my God
Como o tempo voa. How time flies.
soirée evening show
peça play
êxito success
disponível available, free

Tenth lesson/décima lição

45 The personal infinitive

Although this tense is unique to Portuguese, it presents little difficulty to foreigners, for whom it simplifies syntax. In some cases, for instance, it can replace the more complicated subjunctive.

The formation of the personal infinitive is the same for all verbs, without exception. It is an infinitive with personal endings to indicate the person to whom the infinitive refers. It has only one set of endings, whether the verb is regular or irregular, and it can be used with subject pronouns.

The personal infinitive

	SINGULAR	PLURAL
1st person	**eu** falar	falar**mos**
2nd person (familiar)	falar**es**	falar**em**
2nd person (informal)	**você** falar	
3rd person	**ele/ela** falar	falar**em**

Uses of the personal infinitive

1 in place of the subjunctive

The personal infinitive can replace the subjunctive after verbs of commanding, requesting and verbs of emotion provided the conjunction is replaced with a preposition. (See *Uses of the subjunctive mood* in section 40, page 90.) **Que** is removed and in some cases replaced by **de**, as with **antes** and **depois**:

subjunctive:	**Ela pediu para que lhe telefonássemos.**
pers inf:	**Ela pediu para lhe telefonarmos.**
	She asked us to telephone him.

subjunctive:	**Vou sair antes que chova.**
pers inf:	**Vou sair antes de chover.**
	I am going out before it rains.

The personal infinitive can also replace the subjunctive in impersonal expressions and after such verbs as **surpreender, agradar, estranhar, ter pena, lamentar, recear**. In these cases, it requires no preposition:

subjunctive:	**É pena que não estejam aqui.**
pers inf:	**É pena não estarem aqui.**
	It's a shame they are not here.
subjunctive:	**É bom que eles vǎo dar uma volta.**
pers inf:	**É bom irem dar uma volta.**
	It's a good idea for them to go for a walk.

The personal infinitive can replace the subjunctive in adverbial clauses. For example:

subjunctive:	**Partiram sem que lhes disséssemos adeus.**
pers inf:	**Partiram sem lhes dizermos adeus.**
	They left without our saying goodbye to them.
subjunctive:	**Antes que eu chegasse, já ele tinha partido.**
pers inf:	**Antes de eu chegar, já ele tinha partido.**
	Before I arrived, he had already left.

Notice that in the above examples, subordinate clauses containing a subjunctive are always introduced by **que**, whereas those containing a personal infinitive are not.

3 To express 'on doing something'

The personal infinitive is a simple and convenient way of expressing the English construction 'on' + *present participle*. It can be used in combination with past, present and future tenses. For example:

Ao chegarem, encontraram-se logo com o Primeiro Ministro. On arriving, they met the Prime Minister at once.

In English, to avoid ambiguity, we would probably say, 'On their arrival . . .'. But in Portuguese, the ending **em** immediately identifies 'them' as the subject of the personal infinitive. More examples:

Ao entrar, vi o ladrão. On my entering, I spotted the thief.
Só saberei a resposta ao chegar ao escritório. I shall only know the answer on my arriving at the office.

Note: although you may use the subject pronouns with the future tense, it is not common practice to use them after **ao** 'on doing something'.

4 To express the reason for doing something, with por

The personal infinitive is useful as a succinct way of replacing **porque** + *indicative*, as the following examples illustrate.

indicative:	Não te escrevemos porque não sabíamos a tua morada.
pers inf:	Não te escrevemos por não sabermos a tua morada.
	We did not write to you because we did not know your address.
indicative:	Inácio partiu porque chegou a sua sogra.
pers inf:	Inácio partiu por chegar a sua sogra.
	Ignatius departed because his mother-in-law arrived.

5 Idiomatic use to express irony, sarcasm or incredulity

When the personal infinitive is used in this way, the meaning – in speech, at any rate – is likely to be conveyed as much by intonation as by the construction and form of verb. Such expressions can often be translated word for word into English, but are usually best rendered by the use of an extra phrase. Consider these examples:

Tu, estudares? You? Studying? (*or:* What? You're actually studying?)
Nós, mentirmos por causa de você? Us? Tell lies on your account? (*or:* Do you really expect us to tell lies for your sake?)

Exercise 30

Translate the following:
1 Este livro é para lermos.
2 Não quero comprar o carro sem tu concordares.
3 É pena não poderes vir no próximo domingo.
4 Foi bom trazerem os vossos casacos porque vai estar frio.
5 Receio estarem zangados comigo.
6 Não vieram por estarem cansados.
7 Foi impossível irmos à tourada.
8 Vocês, ganharem a taça mundial?
9 They are going to leave before we arrive.
10 It was impossible for us to see the minister.
11 It surprises me your (*familiar*) saying a thing like that.
12 I said good-bye to them before they left.
13 I cannot give an opinion until we know everything.
14 We didn't have lunch because we did not have time.

Vocabulary:

concordar to agree
casaco coat
recear to fear
zangado cross, angry
tourada bullfight
taça mundial world cup (*In Brazil:* **copa do mundo**)
uma coisa assim/uma coisa destas a thing like that

46 The present participle

The present participle is formed by removing the **r** from the infinitive and adding **ndo** to the stem. There are no exceptions.

fala|**r**→fala**ndo**   speaking
come|**r**→come**ndo**   eating
abri|**r**→abri**ndo**   opening

In general, the use of the present participle in Portuguese is much more limited than in English. It cannot be used as a noun. It is used principally in adverbial clauses. For example:

Lá continuaram a sua viagem, passando por aldeias, atravessando rios e subindo montanhas. There they continued their journey, passing through villages, crossing rivers and ascending mountains.

The Portuguese present participle can be used to translate 'on' + *present participle* in English only when the action described by the present participle precedes the action of the verb in the main clause, or when the two actions are simultaneous. For example:

Dizendo isto, desapareceu. On saying this, he disappeared. (So saying, he disappeared.)
Sendo assim, aceito com prazer. This being the case, I will accept with pleasure.

47 Uses of the infinitive

There are some important instances in Portuguese where the infinitive must be used to translate the English present participle.

1 Continuous tenses

In Portuguese, continuous actions are not expressed by the present participle, as they are in English. Instead, the infinitive is used with the appropriate form of **estar a**. Thus we have:

Estou a ler o jornal. I am reading the paper.
Estavam a jogar futebol. They were playing football.

However, when the action takes place over a prolonged period, it is preferable to use **andar a** + *infinitive* instead of **estar a**. For example:

Ando a aprender português. I am learning Portuguese. (I have been learning Portuguese.)
Andam a construir uma nova câmara municipal. They are building a new town hall.

It is also common in Portuguese to use the simple present and imperfect tenses to express continuous action in the present and past respectively. For example:

Aonde vais? Where are you going?
Que fazias? What were you doing?

In Brazilian Portuguese, however, the present participle is used in continuous tenses. Thus it follows the English pattern exactly:

Eles estão jogando futebol. They are playing football.

2 In place of the gerund

In English, when a verb is used as a noun (the gerund), it is the present participle that is used. In Portuguese it is the infinitive that performs this function. For example:

É proibido fumar. No smoking allowed.

48 Por and para

The prepositions **por** and **para** are both used to translate the English 'for' in various situations. Although the general uses given below help to distinguish between uses of **por** and **para**, they are not always easy to apply. It is important, therefore, to observe carefully how they are used in individual cases and to memorise them when the distinction is not clear.

Uses of por

1 On behalf of . . ., on account of . . .

Eu pago a conta por você. I will pay the bill for you. (on your behalf)
Ele lutou por ti. He fought for you. (on your behalf, *or* on your account)

2 In exchange for . . .

Troco este casaco pelo seu chapéu. I will give you this coat for your hat.

3 In expressions of time

Por is used in a number of expressions of time, mainly relating to duration or frequency. When it relates to frequency, it corresponds exactly to the use of 'per' in English:

Eles vieram por duas semanas. They came for two weeks. (duration)
Ele vai a Paris duas vezes por semana. He goes to Paris twice a week.
(frequency)
Pela primeira vez, vi que ela era bonita. For the first time, I noticed that she
was pretty.

4 Por meaning 'by', 'through', 'along' etc

In most contexts, 'by' is translated by **por**. It is also used to translate
'through' and 'along', especially with verbs of motion. It is frequently used
in conjunction with other adverbs to imply motion. The following examples
should help to illustrate this:

Vou pela praia. I am going along the beach.
Viajo a Portugal por França. I travel to Portugal through France.
Vamos pela TAP, naturalmente. We are going by TAP,* of course.
É por aqui ou por ali? Is it this way or that way?
Por onde desapareceu? Where did it disappear to?

*Transportes Aéreos Portugueses (Air Portugal)

Uses of para

1 Destination, purpose

In this case, **para** is used mainly with verbs of motion and in expressions
where giving or sending is implied. For example:

Ele vai para o Brasil. He is going to Brazil.
(The preposition **a** also means 'to' but usually implies that the visit will be
of short duration, whereas **para** implies a longer or permanent stay.)
Estas flores são para ti. These flowers are for you.
Para que faz você isso? What are you doing that for?

2 Expressions of fixed time

Whereas **por** is used to express duration ('time within which . . .') or
frequency, **para** refers to 'time at which . . .' For example:

Tenho hora marcada para as três. I have an appointment for three o'clock.'

3 Imminence 'about'

Os pais dele estão para chegar. His parents are about to arrive.
Estava para comprar um carro alemão, mas mudei de ideias. I was about to
buy a German car, but I changed my mind.

4 Viewpoint

Esse trabalho é muito difícil para mim. This work is very difficult for me.
Este casaco é demasiado grande para ele. This coat is too big for him.

49 The definite article

In previous lessons we have seen that in Portuguese, unlike English, the definite article is required before possessive adjectives. For example:

a minha irmã my sister

However, when the relationship between the possessor and the thing possessed is unmistakably clear – such is the case with parts of the body or personal clothing – the possessive adjective is omitted altogether and only the definite article is used. For example:

O meu pai abanou a cabeça. My father shook his head.
O homem tirou o chapéu. The man took off his hat.

There are a number of occasions when the definite article is used in Portuguese but not in English. The most common of these are listed below.

Names of people: **a Rita, o José** etc

Continents: **a Europa, a Africa** etc

Provinces: **a Estremadura** (south-west Portugal)

Countries: **a Inglaterra** (But Portugal and her former overseas colonies do not require the definite article.)

Cities do not require the article unless they have a physical meaning, as in **o Porto**.

Rivers: **o Tejo** the Tagus, **o Tamisa** the Thames, **o Sena** the Seine.

The definite article is used before **Senhor, Senhora** and **Menina** except in correspondence – in addressing an envelope for example.

In generic expressions: When referring to a class of persons or things in general, the definite article is used. For example:

Os homens cada vez estão mais fracos. Men (in general) are getting weaker and weaker.
Os cães ladram. Dogs (in general) bark.

108

In expressions of time, in combination with the prepositions **em** and **a**:

Na quarta-feira passada last Wednesday
No inverno in winter
Às três horas at three o'clock

Exercise 31
Translate the following:
1 Não tenho tempo para escrever cartas.
2 Ele foi ao Brasil por quatro meses.
3 A minha irmã vai para o hospital na terça-feira para fazer uma operação à garganta.
4 Digo-lhe isto para seu bem.
5 Não foi por querer que o magoei.
6 No mês passado fui a Paris visitar a minha tia.
7 Muito obrigado pela sua amabilidade.
8 Por mim não me importo.
9 I have no news for you (*familiar*)
10 He fought for the rights of Mankind.
11 He has gone to London on business.
12 Are you (*formal*) going home now?
13 If I had my way money would be abolished.
14 I beg your pardon for arriving late.
15 I am going to bed.

Vocabulary:

por querer on purpose
magoar to hurt

COMPREHENSION AND CONVERSATION

Acidentes e incidentes/Accidents and incidents

1 *Problemas com as autoridades locais*

Calculem que recebemos ontem um comunicado da Câmara, um tanto ou quanto ameaçador, porque alguns dos proprietários da aldeia não tinham ainda pago as suas contribuições prediais!

. . . Se eles aceitassem cheques por correio, em vez de quererem que os donos de casa vão lá pessoalmente em dias e horas determinadas, eles não teriam razão de se queixar da falta de pagamento das tais contribuições.

2 *Problemas com a autorização e o visto*

Meu sobrinho chegou ontem do Brasil. Nem o esperávamos. Ele estava lá tão feliz, onde se encontrava há já dois anos, que ficámos admirados quando recebemos um telegrama dizendo que ele vinha. Aparentemente as autoridades brasileiras recusaram-lhe a autorização de trabalho e residência permanente no Brasil. E como o visto terminava depois duma semana disseram-lhe para sair daquele país dentro desse prazo. Foi um grande choque e desilusão para ele, porque tinha lá um bom emprego como arquitecto, e já tinha arranjado um apartamento no Rio de Janeiro, depois de ter procurado muito. Ele vai escrever ao Embaixador a pedir-lhe que o ajude, pois foi sempre o sonho dele viver no Brasil. Além disso ele tem lá namorada.

3 Catástrofes domésticas

a Senhora Valente	Hoje tem sido um daqueles dias de azar. O meu autoclismo recusa-se a funcionar, o cano do lava-louças está entupido e a torneira da banheira continua a pingar sem cessar.
a Senhora Marques	Você tem de chamar um canalizador.
a Senhora Valente	Sim, e não é só ele. A campaínha da porta não toca, não sei porquê. A televisão está avariada e os electricistas estão em greve. A minha mulher a dias não está em greve mas fez gazeta hoje, dizendo que tinha uma grande constipação. E amanhã tenho estes convidados que chegam de Londres para virem passar uma semana connosco. Valha-me Deus! Que vou fazer?
a Senhora Marques	Coitada! Mas não se apoquente desse modo porque não remedeia nada. Eu aconselhava-a a que recebesse os seus convidados muito calmamente e que lhes apresentasse a situação duma maneira cómica. Diga-lhes que o ambiente é primitivo. Os ingleses têm um extraordinário sentido de humor e apreciam muito as pessoas que fazem brincadeira de tudo quanto é aborrecido.

4 O fogo

primeiro veraneante	Socorro! Socorro! Chamem os bombeiros e a ambulância.
segundo veraneante	O que é? Onde é o incêndio?
primeiro veraneante	É ali no mato. está-se a alastrar rapidamente. E oiço crianças a chorarem e pessoas a gritarem. Devem ser famílias que foram lá hoje fazer piquenique. Com um dia tão lindo! E é por isso que as labaredas avançam rapidamente porque está tudo tão seco! Oxalá não haja mortos ou ferimentos graves.
segundo veraneante	Se Deus quiser não haverá. Olhe, cá estão as ambulâncias e os bombeiros. Levaram só dois minutos. São muito competentes!

110

primeiro veraneante Que pena o mato ficar queimado! Tinha árvores tão
antigas e magestosas!
segundo veraneante Possivelmente foi um irresponsável que atirou o
cigarro para o chão, sem pensar nas consequências.

Vocabulary:

1
comunicado report, notice (*in this story* a circular)
câmara municipal offices, the borough authorities
um tanto ou quanto somewhat
ameaçador threatening
proprietários houseowners, landowners
aldeia village
contribuições prediais rates (*local rates for houses*)
por correio by post
em vez de instead of
falta de pagamento failure in payment
tais contribuições the said (the above-mentioned) rates
queixar-se to complain
Note how the imperfect subjunctive is used in the sentence **Se eles
aceitassem**. . ., *and the personal infinitive in* **de quererem**.

2
sobrinho nephew
Nem o esperávamos. We didn't even expect him.
ficamos admirados we were surprised
recusaram-lhe they refused him
visto visa
país country
dentro desse prazo within that given period, time limit
desilusão disappointment
ter procurado depois de after having looked for
embaixador ambassador
além disso besides
namorada girlfriend
ajudar to help
Note the pronunciation of **país** [pe^r-eesh] country *is different from* **pais**
[*pah'*ysh] parents.

3
azar bad luck
autoclismo the flush (*of the cistern*)
o cano do lava-louças the pipe of the sink
entupido blocked
a torneira the tap

banheira the bathtub
pingar to drip, dripping
canalizador plumber
campainha da porta the door bell
tocar to ring (*also* to play music)
A televisão está avariada. The TV is out of order.
em greve on strike
mulher a dias daily woman, charlady
Fez gazeta hoje. She has not turned up today.
uma grande constipação a nasty cold
convidados guests
Valha-me Deus. May God help me.
Coitada! Poor you!
Não se apoquente desse modo. Don't worry yourself like that. Don't upset yourself in this way.
Não remedeia. It does not help. It does not solve anything.
aconselhava I would advise
ambiente environment
sentido de humor sense of humour
fazer brincadeira de to make fun of

4
Socorro! Help!
bombeiros firemen
incêndio fire
mato woods, undergrowth, scrub
alastrar-se to spread
oiço I hear
chorar to cry
gritar to shout, to scream
labaredas flames
avançar to advance
seco dry
mortos dead people (*in this case* deaths)
ferimentos graves serious injuries
se Deus quiser God willing
Olhe! Look!
competente efficient
Que pena! What a shame!
queimado burnt
atirar to throw
cigarro cigarette
chão floor, ground

Reading practice

A menina do mar

—Eu sou uma menina do mar. Chamo-me Menina do Mar e não tenho outro nome. Não sei onde nasci. Um dia uma gaivota trouxe-me no bico para esta praia. Pôs-me numa rocha na maré vaza e o polvo, o caranguejo e o peixe tomaram conta de mim. Vivemos os quatro numa gruta muito bonita. O polvo arruma a casa, alisa a areia, vai buscar a comida. É de nós todos o que trabalha mais, porque tem muitos braços. O caranguejo é o cozinheiro. Faz caldo verde com limos, sorvetes de espuma, e salada de algas, sopa de tartaruga, caviar e muitas outras receitas. É um grande cozinheiro. Quando a comida está pronta o polvo põe a mesa. A toalha é uma alga branca e os pratos são conchas. Depois, à noite, o polvo faz a minha cama com algas muito verdes e muito macias. Mas o costureiro dos meus vestidos é o caranguejo. E é também o meu ourives: ele é que faz os meus colares de búzios, de corais e de pérolas. O peixe não faz nada porque não tem mãos, nem braços com ventosas como o polvo, nem braços com tenazes como o caranguejo. Só tem barbatanas e as barbatanas servem só para nadar. Mas é o meu melhor amigo. Como não tem braços nunca me põe de castigo. É com ele que eu brinco. Quando a maré está vazia brincamos nas rochas; quando está maré alta damos passeios no fundo do mar. Tu nunca foste ao fundo do mar e não sabes como lá tudo é bonito. Há florestas de algas jardins de anémonas, prados de conchas. Há cavalos marinhos suspensos na água com um ar espantado, como pontos de interrogação. Há flores que parecem animais e animais que parecem flores. Há grutas misteriosas azuis-escuras, roxas, verdes e há planícies sem fim de areia fina, branca e lisa. Tu és da terra e se fosses ao fundo do mar morrias afogado. Mas eu sou uma menina do mar. Posso respirar dentro da água como os peixes e posso respirar fora da água como os homens.

—E agora que já contei a minha história leva-me outra vez para o pé dos meus amigos que devem estar aflitíssimos.

O rapaz pegou na Menina do Mar com muito cuidado na palma da mão e levou-a outra vez para o sítio de onde a tinha trazido. O polvo, o caranguejo e o peixe – lá estavam os três a chorar abraçados.

—Estou aqui— gritou a menina do mar.

Taken and abridged from *A Menina do Mar* by Sofia de Melo Breyner, one of the best-known writers of modern Portuguese narrative.

The little girl of the sea

"I am a little girl of the sea. My name is Little Girl of the Sea and I do not have any other name. I don't know where I was born. One day a seagull brought me in its beak to this beach. It put me down on a rock at low tide and the octopus, the crab and the fish took care of me. The four of us live in a beautiful cave. The octopus tidies the house up, smooths the sand and fetches food. He works more than any of us because he has many arms. The crab is the cook. He makes green broth with seaweed, foam ice-cream and algae salad, turtle soup, caviar and many other recipes. He is a great cook. When the meal is ready the octopus sets the table. The table-cloth is a white seaweed and the plates are sea-shells. Later, at night the octopus makes my bed with very soft, very green seaweed. But my dressmaker is the crab. He is also my jeweller: he makes my necklaces out of conch-shells, coral and pearls. The fish does not do anything because he has no hands, nor arms with suckers like the octopus nor arms with pincers as the crab has. He only has fins and the fins are only good for swimming. But he is my best friend. As he does not have any arms he cannot punish me. It is with him that I play. When the tide is out we play on the rocks; when it is high tide we go for strolls on the sea-bed. You have never been to the bottom of the sea and so you have no idea how beautiful everything is there. There are forests of seaweed, gardens of sea-anemones, fields of shells. There are sea-horses hanging in the water, looking perplexed like question marks. There are flowers which look like animals and animals which seem to be flowers. There are mysterious grottos – dark blue, purple, green – and there are endless plains with soft, smooth, white sand. You come from the land and if you went to the bottom of the sea you would drown. But I am a little girl of the sea. I can breathe under the water as the fish do, and out of it like men.

"And now that I have told you my story, please take me back to my friends who must be extremly worried."

The boy picked the Little Girl of the Sea up very carefully in the palm of his hand, and took her back to the place from which he had brought her. The octopus, the crab and the fish – there they were, the three of them crying in each other's arms.

"I am here" shouted the little girl of the sea.

Translated from the original by Maria Fernanda Allen.

114

Dos jornais . . .

Dois cadastrados fugiram do tribunal

Um distúrbio simulado por um detido e sua mulher, no momento em que este se preparava para ser julgado no Tribunal de Paços de Ferreira, veio permitir a sua fuga juntamente com outro detido.

O insólito caso, segundo o «DN» apurou, deu-se na terça-feira, quando Casimiro da Silva de 31 anos, a cumprir uma pena de sete anos na Penitenciária de Coimbra, se preparava para ser julgado no referido tribunal por ter agredido, há cerca de um ano, um guarda prisional na Cadeia Central do Norte.

No mesmo dia, o Tribunal de Paços de Ferreira iria tambem julgar Jaime da Silva de 26 anos, preso em Custóias sob a acusação de ter assaltado uma residência e roubado jóias avaliadas em 400 contos.

Na altura em que o Casimiro aguardava numa sala contígua à sala de audiências o início do julgamento, apareceu a sua mulher, tendo-se estabelecido imediatamente uma cena violenta entre os dois. Aí, os guardas intervieram a separá-los e decidiram encerrar o Casimiro numa cela onde também se encontrava o outro réu.

Pouco depois quando os guardas se dirigiram à cela para trazerem o Casimiro até à sala de audiências, deparou-se-lhes a porta arrombada. Dos detidos nem sinal. No chão, segundo o depoimento dos guardas, encontrava-se abandonado um pé-de-cabra, ferramenta que, no meio da altercação, deve ter sido passada ao Casimiro por sua mulher.

Esta eficiente evasão só não causou grande espanto por Casimiro ser um «especialista» neste domínio. O seu cadastro regista uma série de fugas tal como aconteceu em Custóias, quando saltou o muro da prisão e fugiu no seu próprio automóvel.

Diario de Noticias 17.1.1981

From the newspapers . . .

Two men with prison records escaped from court

A man held in custody, and his wife, faked a disturbance just before his case was due to be heard at the court of Paços de Ferreira, which enabled him to escape together with another detained man.

The unusual occurrence, according to Diario de Noticias, took place on Tuesday when Casimiro da Silva, 31 years old, serving a sentence of seven years at Coimbra prison, was about to be tried in the above-mentioned court for assaulting a prison warder in the Central Northern prison, about a year ago.

The same day, the court at Paços de Ferreira was also going to hear the case of Jaime da Silva, 26 years old, apprehended in Custoias and accused of having broken into a home and stolen jewels worth 400,000 escudos.

While Casimiro waited in a room adjacent to the courtroom for his case to be heard, his wife came in and at once started a violent scene. The guards intervened and decided to lock Casimiro up in a cell already occupied by the other accused.

A little while afterwards, when the warders went to the cell to take Casimiro to the courtroom, they saw the door broken open. Of the detainees – no sign. On the floor, according to the testimony of the warders, there was a crowbar lying abandoned, a tool which must have been passed to Casimiro by his wife during the altercation.

This very efficient escape did not cause great surprise, because Casimiro is already known as a "specialist" in this field. His record shows a series of escapes, like the one which happened in Custoias when he jumped the prison wall and got away in his own car.

From *Diario de Noticias* 17.1.1981, translated by Maria Fernanda Allen.

Portugal e Brasil

Nós brasileiros, melhor do que ninguém, podemos falar sobre Portugal e os portuguêses. Pois é verdade que no tempo das suas descobertas os navegadores portuguêses foram donos de terras em todos os continentes; mas foi no Brasil que ficou realmente a marca do gênio português. Eram eles um povo pequeno, que vivia num pequeno país. E assim mesmo tomaram posse do nosso imenso território e o povoaram. Deram-nos a sua lingua, os seus costumes e a sua religião. Lutavam às vezes com os índios, mas preferiam conviver em paz com eles, juntos fundando novas famílias, povoações e cidades.

Na verdade nós somos o que o português nos fêz. No século passado, quando começaram a chegar ao Brasil as grandes ondas de emigrantes italianos, alemães, árabes, etc., os portuguêses já estavam aqui trabalhando sòzinhos há mais de trezentos anos. O Brasil já tinha então a sua nacionalidade própria, e não mudou mais. Os recém-chegados é que mudaram e foram assimilados.

Fiéis à nossa formação pacífica, somos um povo pacífico. Fizemos a independência, a abolição da escravatura, a república, sem guerra; e fazemos as nossas revoluções quase sem luta ou sem derramar sangue de irmãos. Procurando vencer as dificuldades por meio de entendimentos e não lutando. E podemos dizer que esse amor à compreensão e à paz é a melhor herança que Portugal nos deixou.

From *Modern Portuguese* published in the United States by Alfred A. Knopf Inc., New York and distributed by Random House Inc., New York

Portugal and Brazil

We the Brazilians, better than anyone else, can speak about Portugal and the Portuguese. It is a fact that in the days of maritime exploration the Portuguese navigators were masters of lands in all the continents; but it was really in Brazil that the Portuguese left the mark of their genius.

They were a small nation who lived in a small country. But they took possession of our immense territory and they populated it. They gave us their language, their customs and their religion. Sometimes they fought with the native Indians but they preferred to live in peace with them, together founding new families, villages and cities.

Indeed, we are what the Portuguese made us. Last century, when the great waves of Italian, German and Arab emigrants began to arrive in Brazil, the Portuguese had already been working alone in Brazil for more than three hundred years. Brazil had by then her own identity which stayed the same. It was the newcomers who changed and were assimilated.

Faithful to our peaceful formation, we are a peaceful people. We got our independence, abolished slavery, founded our republic without wars; and we made our revolutions almost without fighting and without spilling our brethren's blood. We try to overcome our difficulties by means of understanding and not conflict. And we can say that this love of understanding and of peace is the best heritage Portugal left us.

Translated by Maria Fernanda Allen.

Letters

Carta comercial em resposta a uma queixa por demora de entrega

Lisboa, 8 de Maio de 19___

Il.^{mos} Srs.
Fonseca & C^a.
Porto

Amigos e Srs.

Venho acusar a recepção da v/ estimada carta de 17 do mês findo, na qual V.S.^{as} se queixam da demora na entrega das mercadorias encomendadas pelo vosso favor de 11 de Agosto.

Não foi por culpa nossa que elas não foram expedidas, mas devido à greve dos trabalhadores da doca, que durou uns 15 dias.

Logo que seja possível darei por telegrama a data do embarque.

Lamentando a inconveniencia que esta demora lhes cause, somos com estima e consideração,

De V.S.^{as}
Atenciosamente

*Assinatura*_____

The alternative to the above is beginning the letter with 'Il.^{mos} Srs.' or 'Ex.^{mos} Srs.' for 'Dear Sirs'. Remove the *s* when addressing one person.

Commercial letter in reply to a complaint about delay in delivery

Lisbon, 8 May 19____

Messrs Fonseca & Co.
Porto

Dear Sirs,

I acknowledge receipt of your [esteemed] letter of the 17th of last month, in which you have complained about the delay in the delivery of the goods you ordered in your letter of the 11th of August.

It was not through any fault of ours that they were not forwarded, but due to a strike by dock workers, which lasted 15 days.

I shall send you a telegram as soon as possible, giving the date of their despatch.

We very much regret and apologise for the inconvenience this delay may cause you, and await your kind orders in the future.

Yours faithfully,

Signature _____

Carta familiar

Londres, 28 de Março de 19___

Querida amiga Antónia,

Recebi a sua estimada carta há já um mês e sinto-me muito envergonhada por não lhe ter escrito ainda.

Acredite que não é falta de amizade ou indiferenca, mas falta de tempo. Tudo parece ter conspirado para que eu não tenha um minuto de vagar.

Além do meu livro que vai agora – e já não é sem tempo – para o prelo, tenho tido pessoas de família na minha casa, uma delas doente; ainda por cima, os exames de admissão ao liceu da minha filha, nos quais, graças a Deus ficou aprovada, e os meus próprios alunos da faculdade também nas vésperas dos seus exames. Em face disto tudo, acho que você vai desculpar-me.

Como estão vocês aí? Quando é o casamento da sua filha? Já sei que tem chovido um pouco em Portugal estas últimas semanas. Ainda bem! Oxalá chova mais porque vocês sofreram uma prolongada seca que deve ter causado grandes prejuízos à agricultura. Aqui, ao contrário, temos tido o Março mais chuvoso deste século. O jardim está ensopado. Estou farta de chuva. Se nós pudéssemos exportar chuva estaríamos ricos, e vocês os portugueses em melhor situação ficariam também.

Agradeço-lhe muito o seu amável convite para irmos a Portugal para sua casa. Vocês são muito gentis e nós estamos muito gratos pelas boas temporadas que já passámos aí. Tanto o meu marido como eu aceitamos esta grande oportunidade de vos ver e de estar nesse belo país. Depois escreverei a confirmar as datas.

A propósito de férias, ouvi, nas notícias desta manhã, que o nosso governo está a pensar em introduzir uma nova taxa de turismo sobre aqueles que vão para o estrangeiro em férias. Calcule! Como se não tivéssemos já tantos impostos neste país. O pobre turista acaba por pagar impostos aqui e no estrangeiro só porque precisa de sol e descanso. Não é justo.

Bem, por hoje termino, cá fico aguardando as suas notícias que me dão sempre tanto prazer e prometo ser mais pontual para a próxima.
Beijinhos aos seus filhos, saudades a sua irmã, cumprimentos ao seu marido, uma festinha para o cão – não me lembro do nome – e para si um grande abraço desta sua amiga sempre grata e sempre ao seu dispor.

Mariana

A letter to a friend

London, 28 March 19__

Dear Antonia

I received your much appreciated letter a month ago and I feel very ashamed at not having written to you yet.

Please believe me (when I say) it is not for lack of friendship nor indifference but because of the shortage of time. Everything seems to have conspired so as to leave me without a moment's rest. Apart from my book which is now – and not before time – going to press, I have been having some family members staying at my place, one of them ill; and on top of everything my daughter's entrance examination for the high school, which she passed, thank goodness, and my own university students about to take their examinations. In the face of all this, I feel sure you are going to forgive me.

How are you all, over there? When is your daughter's wedding? I learnt that there has been some rain in Portugal these last few weeks. I am so glad! I hope it will rain much more as you suffered such a long drought which must have caused great damage to agriculture. By contrast we have been having the wettest March of the century. The garden is soaked. I am fed up with the rain. If we could export rain we would be rich, and you, the Portuguese, would be in a better situation as well.

I thank you very much for your kind invitation for us to go to your home in Portugal. You are both very kind and we are very grateful for the good times we have spent there. Both my husband and I accept this great opportunity to go and see you and to be in that lovely country. I shall write later to confirm the dates.

Speaking of holidays, I heard in the news this morning that the government is thinking of introducing a new tourist tax on those who go abroad for their holidays. Just imagine! As though we don't already have enough taxes in this country. The poor tourist ends up paying taxes here and abroad, and all because he wants to have some sun and rest. It is not fair.

Well, I had better finish now: I shall be awaiting your news which always gives me such pleasure and I promise to be more punctual next time. *Kisses to your children, 'saudades'† to your sister, regards to your husband, a pat for the dog – I can't remember his name – and for you, a big hug from this friend of yours who is always grateful and at your disposal.* With best wishes to you all,

Love,

Mariana

*Between the asterisks is a full translation of the typical ending of a

friendly letter to a Portuguese family. After the asterisks, the conventional English ending is given.

†**Saudades** is a word the Portuguese are very proud of; it is their own word; no other language has quite the same expression. In English the closest is 'longing', 'nostalgia' and the verb 'to miss'. For example: **Tenho saudades de Portugal e de ti.** I am missing Portugal and you.

Idiomatic expressions

Ones linked to certain verbs:

dar

dar horas to strike the hour
dar corda ao relógio to wind (up) the clock/watch
dar baixa ao hospital to be admitted into hospital (for treatment)
O médico deu-lhe alta. The doctor discharged him (from the hospital). *See* **ter**
A janela dá para o mar. The window looks out on the sea.
dar para to have a flair for (anything)
Ela dá para a música. She has a flair for music.
O polícia não deu por isso. The police did not notice it/weren't aware of it/didn't realize it.
dar com to come across, to bump into (someone)
dar-se bem/mal em . . . to be well and happy/unhappy in . . . (a place)
dar-se bem/mal com . . . to get along well/badly with . . . (someone)
dar à luz to give birth
dar por certo to take for granted
Quem me dera! How I wish! Would that I might! (*this is the pluperfect tense of* **dar**)
ao Deus dará aimlessly (left to one's own fate)
dar uma vista de olhos to take a quick look at/through

deixar

Ele deixou de fumar. He stopped smoking.
Deixe-me em paz. Leave me alone.
Ela deixou as cartas para outro dia. She put off (writing) the letters until another day.
Elas deixaram as camas por fazer. They left the beds unmade.

estar

estar para sair to be on the point of going out
O teatro estava às moscas. The theatre was left (*literally*) to the flies (i.e. without customers).
O cinema estava à cunha. The cinema was packed.
O trabalho está por fazer. The work remains undone.

123

A gasolina está pela hora da morte. Petrol has become very expensive.
estar de boa maré/má maré to be in a good mood/bad mood
estar em dia com . . . to be up to date with . . . (correspondence etc)
estar com fome/sede (*in Brazil:sêde*) to be hungry/thirsty
estar com sono/frio/calor to be sleepy/hot/cold
estar com sorte/ciúmes/medo (*in Brazil* **mêdo**) to be lucky/jealous/afraid
estar com pressa/vontade de/razão to be in a hurry/to feel like/to be right

fazer

fazer a barba to shave oneself
fazer anos to have a birthday
Ele faz trinta anos hoje. He is thirty today.
Faz bom/mau tempo. The weather is good/bad.
Ela só faz asneiras. She only makes mistakes.
Você fez muito bem/mal. You did the right/wrong thing.
Nadar faz bem à saúde. Swimming is good for the health.
fazer as vontades de . . . to do the will of/to give into the wishes of someone
Farei o possível. I will do my best.
Que é feito dela? What has happened to her?
fazer-se de bôbo to play dumb
fazer uma viagem to take a trip/to go on a journey

ficar

Este chapéu fica-lhe bem. This hat suits you.
Ele ficou bem no exame. He passed the exam.
Fica para a semana. Let us make it next week.
Fica para a outra vez. We'll make it another time.
Fique descansada. Don't worry, rest assured.
Fico contente. I am so happy. (in respect of some news just learnt)
Isto fica entre nós. This is between us.
Ele ficou sem dinheiro. He was left without money.

ir

ir ter com to go to meet
ir de encontro a to collide with
ir de avião/de autocarro (*in Brazil:* **omnibus**)/**de barco** to fly/to go by bus/boat
ir a pé/a cavalo to walk, to go on foot/to ride
Vai mal de saúde. He is in poor health. (*Also:* **Está muito mal.**)
Como vão? How are you (*pl.*)
Ir a Roma e não ver o Papa. To go Rome and not see the Pope (i.e. to go to a place and not see what the place is famous for; *or* not to accomplish one's mission or purpose.)

Ela vai aos ares. She hits the ceiling/blows up in a rage.
Vamos! Let's go!
Sempre foi a Portugal? Did you go to Portugal (in the end/after all)?

pôr

pôr a mesa to set the table
pôr de castigo to punish
Ela pô-lo na rua. She turned him out of doors. (*Literally* into the street)
pôr-se a to begin to
Ela pôs-se a falar muito depressa. She began to speak hurriedly.
O homem põe e Deus dispõe. Man proposes and God disposes.
sem tirar nem pôr precisely/just like that
o pôr de sol sunset

querer

se quiser if you like
como quiser (queira) as you wish.
sem querer unintentionally
Ela fez por querer. She did it on purpose.
Queira sentar-se. Please sit down.
Quem quer vai, quem não quer manda. If you want a thing done, do it yourself.

ser

É isso mesmo. That's just it.
É sempre assim. It always happens that way.
Como foi que . . .? How did it happen that . . .?
É por minha conta. It's on me. (*i.e.* I will pay the bill.)
a não ser que unless
se eu fosse você . . . if I were you . . .
Seja como fôr . . . Be that as it may (in any case)
tal como deve ser as it should be
É a minha vez. It is my turn.
o ser humano the human being

126

Portuguese equivalents of some English idiomatic expressions:

What is it about? **De que se trata?**
Say no more about it. **Não fale mais nisso.**
Forget about it. **Não pense mais nisso.**
ages ago **há muito tempo**
all at once **de repente**
all the better **tanto melhor**
It is all the same to me. **É-me indiferente./Tanto se me dá.**
as it were/so to speak **por assim dizer**
as you like **como quiser**
to back out (of an agreement or commitment) **faltar ao prometido**
Stop beating about the bush. **Deixe-se de rodeios.**
I hope you will soon be better. **Desejo-lhe as melhoras.**
By the way . . . **A propósito . . .**
How did it come about? **Como aconteceu isso?**
Come on!/Come along!/Let's go! **Vamos!**
to be at ease **pôr-se à vontade/estar à vontade**
Take it easy. **Não se canse.**
to fall asleep **adormecer**
to fall in love **apaixonar-se**
to get dark **escurecer/anoitecer**
It is getting late. **Está a fazer-se tarde** (*in Brazil:* **entardecendo**).
to get the sack **ser despedido**
Get out! **Fora!/Rua!**
How are you getting on? **Como lhe corre a vida?/Como vão as coisas?**
I couldn't get a word in edgeways. **Não consegui abrir a boca./Não abri bico.**
I give in. **Desisto./Dou-me por vencido.**
I give up. **Desisto.**
I am going to get ready. **Vou-me arranjar./Vou-me aprontar.**
going like hot cakes **vendendo-se muito bem**
He is hard up. **Ele está em apuros/sem dinheiro.**
I work hard. **Trabalho muito.**
hard to please **difícil de contentar**
He has hardly said one word. **Ele mal disse uma palavra.**
Help! **Socorro!**
Can't be helped! **Não há remédio!/Que remédio!**
Help yourself! **Sirva-se!**
a long way off **a uma grande distancia**
So long! **Adeus!/Até logo!**
to look after **tomar conta de/olhar por**
to look like **parecer-se com**
to make a mistake **enganar-se**
to make the most of it **tirar o melhor partido**

to make up one's mind **decidir-se a**
Never mind./It does not matter. **Não faz mal./Não tem importância.**
Do you mind? **Importa-se?**
Mind the step! **Cuidado com o degrau!**
Mind your own business. **Meta-se na sua vida./Isto não tem nada a ver consigo.**
to be in a good frame of mind/in a good mood **estar bem disposto**
She does not mince words. **Ela não tem papas na língua.**
more or less **mais ou menos**
to the right **à direita**
to be right **ter razão**
It is all right. **Está bem.**
You haven't the right. **Não tem o direito.**
right and wrong **o bem e o mal**
It serves you right! **É bem feito!**
You don't say!/Don't tell me! **Não me diga!**
to be out of one's senses **perder o juizo**
to drive a person out of his senses **fazer perder a cabeça a . . .**
It does not make any sense. **Não faz sentido nenhum.**
so -so **assim assim**
to take advantage of (to take the opportunity) **aproveitar-se de**
to take (unfair) advantage of **tirar partido de/abusar**
to take a photograph **tirar uma fotografia**
to take place **realizar-se/efectuar-se**
It takes all the fun out of it. **Tira-lhe a graça toda.**
That's up to you. **Isso é consigo.**
Where there's a will there's a way. **Querer é poder.**
against my will **contra minha vontade**
If God wills it. **Se Deus quiser.**
It is not worth while. **Não vale a pena.**

More useful words and phrases

em viagem/travelling

Há uma demora de duas horas. There is a delay of two hours.
O avião está atrasado. The plane is late.
devido ao nevoeiro/greve due to fog/strike
Onde é a alfândega/o Posto de Pronto-Socorro/a saída? Where is the
Customs/the First-Aid Post/the exit?
Tem alguma a coisa a declarar? Have you anything to declare?
Falta-me uma mala. One suitcase of mine is missing.
cinto de segurança safety belt
É proibido fumar. Smoking not allowed.
Sinto-me enjoado/-a. I feel air-sick (sea-sick).
Onde são os lavabos/ é o toilete/é a retrete? Where are the lavatories?
A que horas atracou o barco? What time did the boat arrive?
Os passageiros já estão a desembarcar. The passengers are already
disembarking.
As passagens são caras. The fares (by boat or plane) are expensive.
bagageiro porter.

no comboio/on the train

Quero dois bilhetes de ida e volta para o Porto. I want (would like) two
return tickets for Oporto.
É preciso marcar os lugares? Is it necessary to book the seats?
**De que linha parte e comboio (_in Brazil:_ trem) rápido/correio para
. . .** From which platform does the express train/mail train leave for . . .
É directo ou tenho de mudar (_in Brazil:_ . . . de trocar)? Is it direct or do I
have to change?
vagão-restaurante dining-car
vagão-cama (_in Brazil:_ vagão-dormitório) sleeping car
sala de espera waiting-room
carregador porter
depósito de bagagens left luggage
**O comboio vem à tabela (_in Brazil:_ . . . no horário certo)/atrasado/
adiantado?** Will the train be on time/late/early?
estação dos caminhos de ferro railway station

de carro/by car

auto-estrada motorway

estrada nacional class A road
passagem de nível level crossing
passagem de peões/passadeira pedestrian crossing
sentido único one way
perigo danger
desvio diversion
curva perigosa dangerous bend
estacionamento proibido no parking
trabalhos/obras (*in Brazil:* **trabalhadores**) road works
estação de serviço service station
bomba de gasolina petrol pump
Mostre-me a sua carta de condução (*in Brazil:* **carteira de motorista/carta de direçao**). Show me your driving licence.
matrícula registration number

avarias/car breakdown

Rebentou-me um pneu. One of my tyres has burst.
A bateria esta descarregada. The battery is run down.
afinar os travões (*in Brazil:* **acertar os freios**) to adjust the brakes
Preciso de ar nos pneus. I need air in the tyres.
uma lata de óleo a tin of oil
água no radiador water in the radiator
faróis headlights
tubo de escape exhaust pipe
velas spark plugs
mudanças gears
caixa de velocidades gear-box
embraiagem clutch
pára-brisas windshield
limpa pára-brisas wipers
guarda-lama mud-guard
motor de arranque starting motor
roda sobresselente spare tyre
câmara de ar inner tube
marcha atrás (*in Brazil:* **marcha a ré**) reverse
ponto morto neutral

acidentes/accidents

feridos/mortos injured/dead
Mande chamar o médico. Call for the doctor.
Desmaiou./Está a sangrar. He has fainted./He is bleeding.
A ambulância já vem. The ambulance is on its way.
Embateu em/Chocou com . . . It hit . . . It crashed against . . .
camioneta lorry, coach

carro de bois oxen cart
bicicleta bicycle
Tentava ultrapassar o outro. He was trying to overtake the other.
Ia a grande velocidade. He was going (travelling) at high speed.
Atropelou um cão. He ran over a dog.
O carro derrapou. The car skidded.
rua escorregadiça/escorregadia slippery road
testemunhas witnesses
Ouvi o barulho. I heard the noise.

no consultório médico/at the doctor's (consulting-room)

Estou constipado (*in Brazil:* **resfriado**). I have a cold.
O senhor está com a gripe. You have influenza.
receita/remédios prescription/medicine (medicaments)
Tenho dores de cabeça/das costas/da garganta/da barriga. I have a
head-ache/back-ache/sore throat/tummy-ache.
insolação sun-stroke
intoxicação alimentar food poisoning
enxaqueca migraine
febre fever
Desloquei o braço/o tornozelo. I sprained my arm/my ankle.
Deite-se. Dispa-se. Vista-se. Lie down. Get undressed. Get dressed.
injecções/xarope/comprimidos/pomada/tónico/vitaminas
injections/cough mixture/tablets/ointment/tonic/vitamins
dar baixa ao hospital to go into hospital
Teve alta do hospital. He was discharged from hospital.
Estimo as melhoras. I hope you will get better (soon).
enfermeira/enfermeira-chefe nurse/sister
prisão de ventre/tonturas constipation/dizzy spells
arrepios de frio cold shivers
fraco/a weak

dentista/dentist

dores de dentes toothache
Abra a boca. Open your mouth.
Vou tirar uma radiografia. I am going to take an X-ray.
Precisa de arrancar este dente. You need to have this tooth (pulled) out.
Este dente precisa de ser chumbado. This tooth needs to be filled.
Tem uma cárie. You have a decayed tooth.
Quanto é a consulta? How much is the consultation fee?
Está a doer-me/magoar-me. You are hurting me.

no hotel/at the hotel

A que horas é o pequeno almoço? What time is breakfast (served)?

Pode acordar-me às sete horas? Can you wake me up at seven?
O horário das refeições está no seu quarto. The list of meal times is in your room.
pensão completa/meia-pensão full board/half-board
só dormida room only
quarto de casal com casa de banho (*in Brazil:* **com banheiro**) double room with bathroom
quarto para pessoa só com chuveiro single room with shower
Preciso de uma outra almofada/cobertor. I need another pillow/blanket.
Como se acende/apaga a televisão/a luz? How do you switch on/off the T.V./the light?
Onde se pode alugar um automóvel? Where can one hire a car?
O ar condicionado/aquecimento central está avariado. The air conditioning/central heating is not working (out of order).
Como se abrem os estores? How do you work these blinds?
Estão incluidos o serviço e o imposto? Does that include all service and taxes?
Onde fica a piscina? Where is the swimming-pool?
Tenho uma reclamação/queixa a fazer I have a complaint to make.
Onde está o gerente? Where is the manager?
Gostei da estadia. I enjoyed my stay.
É muito amável. You are very kind.
Obrigado/a pela sua ajuda. Thank you for your help.

no restaurante/in the restaurant

Traga-me a ementa/a conta. Please bring me the menu/the bill.
garrafa de vinho tinto/branco bottle of red/white wine
pão com manteiga/compota bread and butter/jam
torrada toast
O que me recomenda/aconselha? What do you recommend?
prato do dia plate of the day
mal passado/bem passado/picante rare/well-done/spicy
Preciso de sal/pimenta/mustarda. I need salt/pepper/mustard.
Não tenho guardanapo. I haven't a napkin.
Esqueceu-se da salada. You have forgotten the salad.
jarro de água jug of water
Não como carne/peixe. I don't eat meat/fish.
Este copo está sujo. This glass is dirty.
Falta uma faca/uma colher/um garfo. A knife/spoon/fork is missing.
A refeição estava óptima/excelente. The meal was super/excellent.
a gorjeta the tip
Fique com o troco. Keep the change.
Não quero mais. Basta./Chega. I don't want any more. Enough!
um pouco mais a little more

casas e situações domésticas/house and household (domestic situations)

anúncio/venda/compra/renda advertisement/sale/purchase/rent
senhorio/inquilino/notário landlord/tenant/solicitor
escritura/câmara/contribuição predial deeds/town hall/municipality rates
casas assoalhadas/divisões rooms (*not counting kitchen, bathroom*)
Já dei o sinal. I have already given the deposit.
Ela vai mudar-se. She is going to move (house).
orçamento/despesas estimate (budget)/expenses
O autoclismo não funciona. The flush is not working.
A torneira da banheira/do lavatório está a pingar. The tap of the bath/wash-basin is dripping.
Os canos estão entupidos. The pipes are blocked.
A mulher a dias hoje fez gazeta. Today the 'daily' has not turned up.
passar a ferro/engomar to iron
lavar a louça/a roupa to wash up/wash clothes
Não ponha goma nestes colarinhos. Don't starch these (men's) collars.
Esta saia precisa de ser limpa a seco. This skirt needs to be dry-cleaned.
Tem muitas nódoas. It has many stains.
O frigorífico está sujo. The refrigerator is dirty.
Esta mesa deve ser encerada. This table should be polished.
A campaínha da porta não toca. The door bell is not ringing.
quarto/sala de visitas/cozinha bedroom/sitting-room/kitchen
casa de jantar/casa de banho/varanda dining-room/bathroom/balcony
O leite está azedo. The milk has gone sour.
As maçãs estão pôdres. The apples are rotten.
Há falta de batatas. There is a shortage of potatoes.
Quero que me descasques estas cebolas. I want you to peel these onions for me.
Vou descascar estas laranjas. I am going to peel these oranges.
Os padeiros estão em greve. The bakers are on strike.
Havia uma grande bicha (*in Brazil:* **fila**) **no talho.** There was a long queue at the butcher's.

compras em geral/shopping (in general)

drogaria drugstore
mercearia grocer
tabacaria tobacconist
Quero dois maços de cigarros ingleses. I want two packets of English cigarettes.
De que marca? Which brand?
Quanto custa? How much is it?
caixa/carteira de fósforos box/book of matches
postais ilustrados/revista/jornal postcards/magazine/newspaper
rolo a cores (*in Brazil:* **filme em cores**) colour film

rolo a preto e branco (*in Brazil:* **filme em . . .**) black and white film
Onde se pode mandar revelar? Where can one have it developed?
Onde fica a esquadra/o posto de polícia? Where is the police station?
estação dos correios/selos/via aérea post-office/stamps/by air mail
impressos para telegramas/vale postal forms for telegrams/postal money
order
Onde se levantam as encomendas postais? Where does one collect
registered parcels?
sapataria shoe-shop
Estes sapatos não me servem. These shoes do not fit me.
Qual é o tamanho/o número que calça/que veste? What size/number do you
take in shoes/clothes?
salto alto/salto baixo/salto raso high heel/low heel/flat heel
secção de retrosaria/de chapelaria department of haberdashery/millinery
tecidos/fazenda/seda (*in Brazil:* **sêda**)/**algodão/lã** materials/woollen cloth/
silk/cotton/wool
Este casaco (*in Brazil:* **paletó**) **está-me apertado.** This coat is tight on me.
Esta cor (*in Brazil:* **côr**) **não me fica bem.** This colour does not suit me.

roupa or vestuário e cores/clothes and colours

fato (*in Brazil:* **terno**)/**saia/casaco** suit/skirt/coat (jacket)
vestido/calças/calções (*in Brazil:* **calças de esporte**) dress/trousers/shorts/
fato de banho (*in Brazil:* **maiô de banho**) swimsuit
sobretudo/camisola/blusa/lenço overcoat/jumper/blouse/handkerchief
impermeável/guarda-chuva/cinto/luvas raincoat/umbrella/belt/gloves
cinta/meias/cuecas/soutien girdle/stockings/pants/bra
peúgas/camisa de noite (*in Brazil:* **camisola**)/**roupa de interior**
socks/nightdress/underclothes
gravata/pijama/colete/camisa tie/pyjamas/waistcoat/shirt
verde/azul/branco/preto/roxo green/blue/white/black/purple
encarnado/vermelho/amarelo red/dark red/yellow
cinzento/castanho (*in Brazil:* **marron**)/**côr-de-rosa** grey/brown/pink
côr-de-laranja/claro/escuro/dourado orange/light/dark/gold
prateado/beige/côr de camelo/creme silver/beige/camel colour/cream

cabeleireiro, barbeiro/hairdresser, barber

Quero uma mise/permanente/pintura (*in Brazil:* **tintura**). I want a
set/perm/tint.
um penteado simples/elegante a simple/elegant hairstyle
um corte/só aparado/ripado (*in Brazil:* **desfiado/a unhas feitas**) a cut/only
trimmed/back-combed
Deixe-o comprido/curto. Leave it long/short.
Tenho o cabelo encaracolado/ondulado/liso. I have curly/wavy/straight hair.

Não quero o cabelo frisado. I don't want my hair frizzy.
Quanto tempo preciso de ficar debaixo do secador? How long do I need to be under the dryer?
Quero as minhas unhas arranjadas. I want my nails done.
Quero só fazer a barba. I just want a shave.
Não toque no bigode ou nas suiças/patilhas. Don't touch the moustache or side-whiskers/sideburns.
Faça o risco ao lado/ao meio. Part it on the side/centre.

divertimentos/entertainment and pastimes

corrida de cavalos/de bicicleta horse race/bicycle race
tourada/toureiro/espada/perícia bullfight/bullfighter/sword/skill
desafio de futebol (*in Brazil:* **jogo de futebol**)**/empate** football match/draw
jogar as cartas/o xadrez/apostar to play cards/chess/to bet
bilheteira/lotação esgotada (*in Brazil:* **bilheteria/ingressos esgotados**) ticket office/house sold out
barco à vela/à motor/remar sailing boat/motor boat/to row
corte de ténis (*in Brazil:* **quadra de ténis**) tennis court
campo de golfe golf course

Appendix: Verbs

Regular, radical-changing, irregular, and verbs requiring a preposition

Revision table of regular verbs

(only the endings are given)

Indicative mood

PRESENT TENSE			PAST DEFINITE			IMPERFECT		
-ar	**-er**	**-ir**	**-ar**	**-er**	**-ir**	**-ar**	**-er**	**-ir**
-o	-o	-o	-ei	-i	-i	-ava	-ia	-ia
-as	-es	-es	-aste	-este	-iste	-avas	-ias	-ias
-a	-e	-e	-ou	-eu	-iu	-ava	-ia	-ia
-amos	-emos	-imos	-ámos	-emos	-imos	-ávamos	-íamos	-íamos
-am	-em	-em	-aram	-eram	-iram	-avam	-iam	-iam

FUTURE*			CONDITIONAL*			*Past participle*		
-ar	**-er**	**-ir**	**-ar**	**-er**	**-ir**	**-ar**	**-er**	**-ir**
-ei	-ei	-ei	-ia	-ia	-ia	-ado	-ido	-ido
-ás	-ás	-ás	-ias	-ias	-ias			
-á	-á	-á	-ia	-ia	-ia			
-emos	-emos	-emos	-íamos	-íamos	-íamos			
-ão	-ão	-ão	-iam	-iam	-iam			

(used in forming compound tenses, such as the perfect, pluperfect and others)

Subjunctive mood

PRESENT			IMPERFECT			FUTURE**		
-ar	**-er**	**-ir**	**-ar**	**-er**	**-ir**	**-ar**	**-er**	**-ir**
-e	-a	-a	-asse	-esse	-isse	-ar	-er	-ir
-es	-as	-as	-asses	-esses	-isses	-ares	-eres	-ires
-e	-a	-a	-asse	-esse	-isse	-ar	-er	-ir
-emos	-amos	-amos	-ássemos	-êssemos	-íssemos	-armos	-ermos	-irmos
-em	-am	-am	-assem	-essem	-issem	-arem	-erem	-irem

Imperative

-ar	**-er**	**-ir**	
-a	-e	-e	(you, *familiar*)
-e	-a	-a	(you, *formal*)
-emos	-amos	-amos	(let us . . .)
-ai	-ei	-i	(you, *plural, classical language*)
-em	-am	-am	(you, *plural*)

Present participle

-ar	**-er**	**-ir**
-ando	-endo	-indo

NOTES:

*When forming the future and conditional of the indicative mood, the endings given above are added to the infinitive, without removing its

136

ending: e.g. fal|ar|ei, fal|ar|ia. In the other tenses, the infinitive endings (-ar, -er, -ir) are dropped: fal|o, fal|ei, etc.
**The personal infinitive of these regular verbs is formed in the same way as the future of the subjunctive, given above.

Radical-changing verbs

The stem of the infinitive changes only in the 1st person singular of the present tense indicative and consequently in all persons of the subjunctive.

e to i

INFINITIVE	PRESENT TENSE	PRESENT SUBJUNCTIVE
seguir (to follow)	sigo	siga, -as, -a, -amos, -am
preferir (to prefer)	prefiro	prefira etc
mentir (to lie)	minto	minta etc
vestir (to dress)	visto	vista etc
servir (to serve)	sirvo	sirva etc
sentir (to feel)	sinto	sinta etc
divertir-se (to enjoy)	divirto-me	me divirta etc
despir (to undress)	dispo	dispa etc
conseguir (to succeed, manage, achieve)	consigo	consiga etc
repetir (to repeat)	repito	repita etc

o to u

cobrir (to cover)	cubro	cubra etc
descobrir (to discover)	descubro	descubra etc
dormir (to sleep)	durmo	durma etc
tossir (to cough)	tusso	tussa etc

But verbs **subir** (to climb, to go up), **fugir** (to run away, to flee), **destruir** (to destroy) and **construir** (to build) have the following changes in the present indicative, e.g.:

eu subo	nós subimos
tu sobes	sobem
ele sobe	

Other radical-changing verbs, which alter in the 1st person singular and subjunctive only:

perder (to lose)	perco	perca etc
medir (to measure)	meço	meça etc
valer (to be worth)	valho	valha etc
pedir (to ask for)	peço	peça etc
ouvir (to hear, listen)	ouço	ouça etc

Spelling-change verbs

The term 'orthographical-changing' is used to describe verbs in which the last consonant of the stem is modified or changed in certain persons and tenses in order to preserve the sound of the infinitive. The most common examples are as follows:

-car→**qu** before **e** or **i**
brin**c**ar (to play)→brin**qu**ei (I played)

-çar→**c** before **e** or **i**
come**ç**ar (to begin)→come**c**ei (I began)

-cer→**ç** before **a**, **o** or **u**
conhe**c**er (to know)→conhe**ç**o (I know)

-gar→**gu** before **e** or **i**
che**g**ar (to arrive)→che**gu**e (I arrived)

-ger', -gir→**j** before **a**, **o** or **u**
fu**g**ir (to flee)→fu**j**o (I flee)

-guer, -guir→**g** before **a**, **o** or **u**
perse**gu**ir (to pursue)→perse**g**o (I pursue)

Table of irregular verbs

In order to make it easier for the student to learn these verbs, we are giving them in order of similarity, where applicable. Only the 1st person singular is given in those tenses (imperfect, future etc) where the *endings* are the same as for the regular tenses.

dar	**estar**	**ser**	**ir**
(*to give*)	(*to be*)	(*to be*)	(*to go*)
PRESENT TENSE			
dou	estou	sou	vou
dás	estás	és	vais
dá	está	é	vai
damos	estamos	somos	vamos
dão	estão	são	vão
PAST DEFINITE			
dei	estive	fui	fui
deste	estiveste	foste	foste
deu	esteve	foi	foi
demos	estivemos	fomos	fomos
deram	estiveram	foram	foram

IMPERFECT

dava	estava	era	ia

FUTURE

darei	estarei	serei	irei

CONDITIONAL

daria	estaria	seria	iria

PRESENT SUBJUNCTIVE

dê	esteja	seja	vá
dês	estejas	sejas	vás
dê	esteja	seja	vá
dêmos	estejamos	sejamos	vamos
dêem	estejam	sejam	vão

IMPERFECT SUBJUNCTIVE

desse	estivesse	fosse	fosse

FUTURE SUBJUNCTIVE

der	estiver	for	for

PERSONAL INFINITIVE

dar	estar	ser	ir
dares	estares	seres	ires
dar	estar	ser	ir
darmos	estarmos	sermos	irmos
darem	estarem	serem	irem

IMPERATIVE

dá	está	sê	vai
dê	esteja	seja	vá
dêmos	estejamos	sejamos	vamos
(dai)	(estai)	(sede)	(ide)
dêem	estejam	sejam	vão

PAST PARTICIPLE

dado	estado	sido	ido

PRESENT PARTICIPLE

dando	estando	sendo	indo

ter	vir	ver	pôr
(to have)	(to come)	(to see)	(to put)

PRESENT TENSE

tenho	venho	vejo	ponho
tens	vens	vês	pões
tem	vem	vê	põe
temos	vimos	vemos	pomos
têm	vêm	vêem	põem

PAST DEFINITE

tive	vim	vi	pus
tiveste	vieste	viste	puseste
teve	veio	viu	pôs
tivemos	viemos	vimos	pusemos
tiveram	vieram	viram	puseram

IMPERFECT

tinha	vinha	via	punha

FUTURE

terei	virei	verei	porei

CONDITIONAL

teria	viria	veria	poria

PRESENT SUBJUNCTIVE

tenha	venha	veja	punha

IMPERFECT SUBJUNCTIVE

tivesse	viesse	visse	pusesse

FUTURE SUBJUNCTIVE

tiver	vier	vir	puser

PERSONAL INFINITIVE

ter	vir	ver	pôr

IMPERATIVE

tem	vem	vê	põe
tenha	venha	veja	ponha
tenhamos	venhamos	vejamos	ponhamos
tende	vinde	(vede)	(ponde)
tenham	venham	vejam	ponham

PAST PARTICIPLE

tido	vindo	visto	posto

PRESENT PARTICIPLE

tendo	vindo	vendo	pondo

trazer	**dizer**	**fazer**	**saber**	**haver**	**poder**
(*to bring*)	(*to say*)	(*to do, make*)	(*to know*)	(*to have*)	(*to be able to*)

PRESENT TENSE

trago	digo	faço	sei	hei	posso
trazes	dizes	fazes	sabes	hás	podes
traz	diz	faz	sabe	há	pode
trazemos	dizemos	fazemos	sabemos	havemos	podemos
trazem	dizem	fazem	sabem	hão	podem

PAST DEFINITE

trouxe	disse	fiz	soube	houve	pude
trouxeste	disseste	fizeste	soubeste	houveste	pudeste
trouxe	disse	fez	soube	houve	pôde
trouxemos	dissemos	fizemos	soubemos	houvemos	pudemos
trouxeram	disseram	fizeram	souberam	houveram	puderam

IMPERFECT

trazia	dizia	fazia	sabia	havia	podia

FUTURE

trarei	direi	farei	(*regular*)	(*regular*)	(*regular*)
trarás	dirás	farás			
trará	dirá	fará			
traremos	diremos	faremos			
trarão	dirão	farão			

CONDITIONAL

traria	diria	faria	(*regular*)	(*regular*)	(*regular*)
trarias	dirias	farias			
traria	diria	faria			
traríamos	diríamos	faríamos			
trariam	diriam	fariam			

PRESENT SUBJUNCTIVE

traga	diga	faça	saiba	haja	possa
tragas	digas	faças	saibas	hajas	possas
traga	diga	faça	saiba	haja	possa
tragamos	digamos	façamos	saibamos	hajamos	possamos
tragam	digam	façam	saibam	hajam	possam

IMPERFECT SUBJUNCTIVE

trouxesse	dissesse	fizesse	soubesse	houvesse	pudesse

FUTURE SUBJUNCTIVE

trouxer	disser	fizer	souber	houver	puder

PERSONAL INFINITIVE

trazer	dizer	fazer	saber	haver	poder

PAST PARTICIPLE

trazido	dito	feito	sabido	havido	podido

PRESENT PARTICIPLE

trazendo	dizendo	fazendo	sabendo	havendo	podendo

IMPERATIVE

traz (e)	diz (e)	faz (e)	sabe	há	pode
traga	diga	faça	saiba	haja	possa
tragamos	digamos	façamos	saibamos	hajamos	possamos
(trazei)	(dizei)	(fazei)	(sabei)	(havei)	(podei)
tragam	digam	façam	saibam	hajam	possam

ler	**crer**	**querer**	**rir***	**caber**
(to read)	*(to think, believe)*	*(to want)*	*(to laugh)*	*(to fit in, be contained)*

PRESENT TENSE

leio	creio	quero	rio	caibo
lês	crês	queres	ris	*(otherwise*
lê	crê	quer(e)	ri	*conjugated*
lemos	cremos	queremos	rimos	*like* saber *in*
lêem	crêem	querem	riem	*all tenses)*

PAST DEFINITE

li	cri	quis	ri
leste	creste	quiseste	riste
leu	creu	quis	riu
lemos	cremos	quisemos	rimos
leram	creram	quiseram	riram

IMPERFECT

lia	cria	queria	ria

FUTURE

lerei	crerei	quererei	rirei

CONDITIONAL

leria	creria	quereria	riria

PRESENT SUBJUNCTIVE

leia	creia	queira	ria

IMPERFECT SUBJUNCTIVE

lesse	cresse	quisesse	risse

FUTURE SUBJUNCTIVE

ler	crer	quiser	rir

PERSONAL INFINITIVE

ler	crer	querer	rir

PAST PARTICIPLE

lido	crido	querido	rido

PRESENT PARTICIPLE

lendo	crendo	querendo	rindo

IMPERATIVE

lê	crê	quer(e)	ri
leia	creia	queira	ria
leiamos	creiamos	queiramos	riamos
(lede)	crede	querei	ride
leiam	creiam	queiram	riam

* **Sorrir** to smile, is conjugated like **rir**.

Some remarks

1 The SIMPLE PLUPERFECT may be encountered in writing but is seldom used in speech, when the compound pluperfect (**tinha falado**) is preferred. In regular verbs you add **ra** to the stem of the infinitive: e.g. **falara**, **comera**, **partira**.
In irregular verbs you add the same termination to the stem of the past definite as for the imperfect and future of the subjunctive mood: e.g. **dissera**, **fizera**, **fora**, **dera**, **trouxera**, **vira**, **tivera**.

2 The subjunctive mood also has its own compound tenses: the perfect, **tenha falado**, the pluperfect, **tivesse falado**, and the compound future, **tiver falado**.

3 Haver is an auxiliary verb which sometimes replaces the verb **ter** in compound tenses, especially in literary works. It is then fully conjugated as shown above.
Haver as an *impersonal verb* only uses the 3rd person singular in all tenses, i.e. **há**, which means 'there is' and 'there are' etc.

Some verbs which require a preposition before the infinitive of another verb

acabar de to finish (doing something)	Acabo de comer. i.e. 'I have just (finished) eaten'.
aconselhar a to advise	Aconselho-o a ver o médico.
ajudar a to help	Ela ajuda-me a lavar a louça.
acabar por to end up (doing . . .)	Ele acabou por consentir.
começar a to begin	Ele começou a falar.
começar por to begin by . . .	Ele começou por dizer.
esquecer-se de to forget	Esqueci-me de te dizer que . . .
lembrar-se de to remember	Não me lembro do seu nome.
gostar de to like	Gosto de comer. (*preposition also needed before a noun*)
obrigar a to force, to compel	Obriguei-a a dizer a verdade.
precisar de to need	Preciso de falar com ele. (*also needed before a noun*)
voltar a (to do it) again	Voltei a vê-lo.
voltar para to return to (do something)	Voltei para te ver.
pensar em to think of	Pensei em falar contigo.
pedir para to ask (to)	Pedi-lhe para fazer isso.

Some verbs followed by a preposition

assistir a to attend	Assisti a uma tourada.
aproximar-se de to go near	Aproximei-me dele.
casar-se com to get married	Ela casou-se com um inglês.
chegar a to arrive at	Cheguei à conclusão. Cheguei a Faro.
dar com to come across, to bump into	Dei com a Manuela no armazém.
dar por to notice	Não dei por ela.
dar para to overlook	O meu quarto dá para o jardim.
acreditar em to believe	Acredito em ti.
duvidar de to doubt	Duvido da sua palavra.
encontrar-se com to meet (by arrangement, mostly)	Vou-me encontrar com eles.
ir a, ir para to go to	Vou a Paris em negócios. (**ir a** *implies a shorter stay than* **ir para**)
olhar para to look, at	Ele olhou para mim.
parecer-se com to look like, resemble	Ela parece-se com o pai.
pegar em to pick up (*In Brazil:* **pegar** *without preposition*)	Ele pegou na mala.
queixar-se de to complain about	Eu queixei-me da comida.

reparar em to notice — Reparei no teu vestido.
sonhar com to dream of — Sonhei contigo.
sorrir para to smile at — Ela sorriu para a menina.
vir a, vir para to come — Ele veio a Londres. (**vir a** *implies a shorter stay than* **vir para**).

Key to Exercises

LESSON 1

Exercise 1: 1 A rapariga. 2 O rapaz. 3 O escritório. 4 A casa. 5 As flores. 6 Os empregos. 7 Os gatos. 8 As alunas.

Exercise 2: 1 Uma viagem. 2 Um escritório. 3 Um avião. 4 Uma cidade. 5 Um bilhete. 6 Uns homens. 7 Umas mulheres. 8 Umas viagens. 9 Uns escritórios. 10 Umas raparigas.

Exercise 3: 1 I have. 2 Have you? 3 We don't have. 4 You have (*pl*). 5 Has she? 6 You do not have (*pl formal*). 7 Não tenho dinheiro. 8 A senhora tem um bilhete? 9 Eles têm bons empregos. 10 Vocês têm uma casa? 11 Tu tens um escritório. 12 Temos fome. 13 Há uma mesa. 14 Há quanto tempo fala inglês?

LESSON 2

Exercise 4: 1 Sou inglesa. 2 O senhor é o gerente deste hotel? 3 Ele é aborrecido. 4 Ela é uma secretária. 5 Isto é muito importante. 6 Nós somos amigas. 7 Eles são velhos. 8 São estas as malas? 9 These suitcases are not mine. 10 This is impossible. 11 I am not a secretary, I am a teacher. 12 We are friends. 13 Are you (*pl informal*) married?

Exercise 5: 1 Estou em Londres. 2 Tu estás cansada? 3 Ela não está em casa. 4 Estamos a trabalhar todos os dias. 5 Eles estão enganados. 6 O combóio (*in Brazil:* trem) está atrasado. 7 I am eating. 8 Are you at home today? 9 We are not mistaken. 10 You (*sing. formal*) are hungry. 11 They are looking beautiful. 12 The girls are ready.

Exercise 6: 1 O livro está na mesa. 2 A mulher esta à porta. 3 Ela vai pelo parque. 4 O escritório do tio Tomás. 5 Estou ao telefone. 6 We are going to the market. 7 I am going home. 8 She is in the bathroom. 9 In a situation like this (one). 10 He came in through the window. 11 I am speaking of the accident. 12 He gave the money to the boy.

LESSON 3

Exercise 7: 1 We are looking for a house. 2 They don't speak Portuguese very well, but they understand everything. 3 She never accepts my invitation. 4 What (will) you take? 5 She opens the window. (She is opening the window.) 6 I study every day. 7 You (*pl informal*) don't eat much. 8 I am leaving at 9 o'clock.

Exercise 8: 1 Meu irmão procura um emprego em Moçambique. 2 Ele aprende português. 3 Precisa de ajuda? 4 Aceito o seu convite com prazer. 5 Bebem e fumam demasiado. 6 O combóio parte à tabela. (*in Brazil:* O trem parte no horário certo.) 7 Ele vende o carro. 8 Hoje não compro nada. 9 Minha irmã não come à uma hora. 10 Ela está de dieta.

Exercise 9: 1 Which is the nearest station from here? 2 What is your address? 3 What time is it? 4 She never does what I want. 5 Why don't you go by car? 6 I believe it is very far. 7 How is business going? - 8 Where are you going? 9 When do they go to Lisbon? 10 How much do I owe?

Exercise 10: 1 That shop on the corner. 2 We are going to that beach. 3 What is this? 4 This is a computer. 5 Please shut that door. 6 This is my husband and that is my son. 7 These keys are not mine. 8 He is in that hotel. 9 This suitcase belongs to that gentleman. 10 Esta casa é grande. 11 O que é isso? 12 Não quero aqueles livros. 13 Isto é impossível. 14 Estes homens são ingleses.

LESSON 4

Exercise 11: 1 I like your home/house very much. 2 This is your glass and that one (over there) is his. 3 Your daughter is very nice/charming. 4 Our holidays begin in June. 5 My wife always arrives late. 6 São estas as suas malas? 7 O meu telefone está sempre avariado. 8 Isto não é meu. 9 Não sei o nome deles. 10 A vossa casa é muito longe. 11 A nossa filha chega amanhã. 12 O amigo dele é americano.

Exercise 12: 1 I finish work/(working) at six o'clock. 2 We are going to spend a fortnight on the beach. 3 She has four brothers (*also meaning* brothers and sisters). 4 The book costs twenty escudos. 5 This lift only takes five people. 6 I go to Paris every four weeks. 7 Ele começa o trabalho às oito horas. 8 Ele tem dois rapazes e três raparigas. 9 Escrevo à minha mãe de cinco em cinco dias. 10 Ele parte a vinte de Maio (*or* Ele parte no dia vinte de Maio). 11 Você come à uma hora? 12 Ele não trabalha há dez dias. 13 Tenho trinta e cinco anos. 14 São seis menos um quarto.

Exercise 13: 1 Next week I am going (I go) to my aunt's (house). 2 Last month my brother went to work in Brazil. 3 My children (sons) will arrive in a fortnight (in 15 days' time). 4 Tonight we are going to the theatre. 5 Spring is my favourite season. 6 Yesterday it was very cold. 7 The day after tomorrow we shall have the results of our examinations. 8 Vou passar o Natal com os meus amigos em Lisboa. 9 Este ano não tenho férias. 10 Ela vai passar o verão no Algarve. 11 Ontem esteve (fez) calor. 12 Faço anos no domingo. 13 Amanhã de manhã começo o trabalho (começo a trabalhar). 14 Julho, Agosto e Setembro são meses muito quentes em Portugal.

LESSON 5

Exercise 14: 1 Hoje o tempo está mau. 2 Ela é uma boa secretária. 3 Não sei onde está o meu mapa francês. 4 Minha irmã é mais velha do que eu. 5 A minha amiga é espanhola, mas o marido dela é inglês. 6 É uma boa coisa que você faz. 7 Há muitas pessoas simpáticas neste mundo (*or* Há muita gente simpática neste mundo). 8 O meu colega está muito contente no Brasil. 9 O Mercado Comum é uma comunidade europeia. 10 A mãe da minha amiga é (uma) poetisa. 11 Tenho um grande carro verde. 12 Meu primo é um bom escritor e a mulher dele é também uma boa escritora. 13 O António é um jornalista português. - 14 Esta galinha está crua.

Exercise 15: 1 Duas salas. 2 Meus irmãos. 3 As flores são lindas. 4 Estes problemas são difíceis. 5 No verão há muita gente nas praias. 6 Três estudantes ingleses. 7 Quatro lençóis. 8 Os meus amigos são muito amáveis. 9 Não conheço estes homens. 10 As crianças alemãs não gostam de cães. 11 Compro cinco pães todos os dias. 12 Ela gosta de todos os animais. 13 A minha irmã tem olhos azuis. 14 Tenho as mãos sujas. 15 Os limões são bons para a saúde. (*also* Os limões fazem bem à saúde.) 16 Meus pais estão sempre tão felizes / contentes.

Exercise 16: 1 Yesterday I received a letter from my friend. 2 We liked your home very much. 3 Last week we visited a very modern school. 4 They have left for Brazil. 5 Have you sold your house yet (already)? 6 No, we haven't sold our house yet. 7 They haven't written yet. 8 Não compreendi. 9 O que beberam eles? 10 Já comi. 11 Quando partiram eles? 12 A que horas partiu o combóio? 13 Não abrimos a janela. 14 Ele não comeu ontem à noite. 15 Você falou com a sua mãe? 16 Conheci o seu irmão em Lisboa.

Exercise 17: 1 Come here. 2 Speak slowly. 3 Don't make a noise. 4 Go that way. 5 Don't be silly. 6 Be still. 7 Bring the wine list. 8 Fale devagar. 9 Abramos a janela. 10 Fechem a porta. 11 Não comam tão depressa. 12 Vejamos . . . . 13 Venham já. 14 Vamos! 15 Não falem tão alto. 16 Não diga nada.

LESSON 6

Exercise 18: 1 Give him/her my regards. 2 She rang me up last night. 3 She/he saw him last week. 4 I don't know them well. 5 They visit us every year. 6 We want to see him. 7 I am going to help you/her. 8 You (*pl*) help him very much. 9 He does not want the apples but I am going to give them to him. 10 You live near me. 11 I don't eat (I shan't eat, I am not eating) without you. 12 Come with me now to have a coffee and then (afterwards) I'll come with you to the hairdresser. 13 The dogs are with us, but the cats are with them (*f*). 14 Who told you that? (Who told it to you?)

Exercise 19: 1 Mostre-nos o que encontrou (achou). 2 Vá procurá-la. (*in Brazil:* Vá buscar a ela.) 3 Estas flores são para mim? 4 Antes que me esqueça tenho de lhes dizer . . .. 5 Ele esperou por nós. 6 Venha comigo. 7 Não há segredos entre nós. 8 Conto contigo. 9 Ele não mo emprestou. 10 Eles ajudam-no. 11 Minha mãe não me telefonou. - 12 Não preciso dele. 13 Chamei-o mas ele não me ouviu. 14 Vi-os a semana passada. 15 Ele vai vê-la.

Exercise 20: 1 When I was a child I learnt everything more easily. (. . . it was easier to learn.) 2 I used to eat a lot, (Before, I ate a lot,) but not now. 3 We used to go to the beach every day. 4 Yesterday we went to the country. 5 It was underneath this tree that I used to sit. 6 What were you doing? 7 I was taking a bath. 8 A que horas tomou o seu pequeno-almoço? 9 Dizia-me por favor onde é (fica) a paragem do autocarro (*in Brazil:* a parada do ônibus?) 10 Soube que o seu irmão ía para a Africa, é verdade? 11 Chovia a cântaros quando saímos. 12 Ele ouvia enquanto eu falava. 13 Já comia. 14 Ontem (à noite) jantei com a minha sogra.

LESSON 7

Exercise 21: 1 Do you want (to take/to have) tea or coffee? 2 I want neither tea nor coffee – I prefer an orange juice. 3 I either go to the cinema or stay at home watching television, I am not sure yet. 4 I have never seen an exhibition so well organized. 5 He has no scruples at all. - 6 I shall never again buy electrical items (appliances) second hand. 7 You have nothing to do with it. (*also:* It is none of your business.) 8 No-one speaks English here. 9 I don't know anything. 10 We did not go anywhere.

Exercise 22: 1 Alguém aqui fala inglês? 2 O senhor pediu-me uma colher ou uma faca? 3 Nem uma nem outra, pedi-lhe um garfo. 4 Ele tem algumas esperanças. 5 Cada qual tem o seu gosto. 6 Está tudo caríssimo. 7 Tem quaisquer revistas inglesas? 8 São ambos escritores. 9 O jantar estava péssimo. 10 A minha tia está muito mal. 11 Ele é o homem mais rico do mundo. 12 Tenho boas noticias para si. 13 Ela está tão feliz como eu. 14 Camões foi o maior poeta português.

Exercise 23: 1 Quando lhe escreverá? (*also:* Quando lhe vai escrever?) 2 Ele tem de trabalhar muito. 3 Não o tomaremos. 4 Começarei a minha história. 5 Quem ganhará? 6 Chegaremos no próximo mês. 7 Seria a verdade? 8 I should say he is lying. 9 I shall not forget you. 10 I would do everything for her. 11 They will give him/her/you my new address. 12 I will go to Japan. 13 I have to go to the dentist. 14 Will it be very expensive?

LESSON 8

Exercise 24: 1 She had already studied Portuguese when she was a child.

2 This year there have been many plane accidents. 3 The woman was already dead when the doctor arrived. 4 The tables were already laid but the guests had not arrived yet. 5 I had never seen so many people in my life. 6 She was expelled from the school. 7 It is said (They say) that the firm (Messrs) Agiota & Co. is going bankrupt. 8 One must not deceive (cheat, mislead) others. 9 They had not washed themselves yet. (They had not had a wash.) 10 The weather has been bad.

Exercise 25: 1 They felt (were) disappointed. 2 I got up very early. 3 He never remembers my birthday. 4 She got dressed in a hurry. 5 He smells awful because he never washes himself. (. . . he never has a wash.) 6 How do you say 'table' in Portuguese? 7 They looked at each other. 8 Help yourself while the food is hot. 9 We don't know each other. 10 I complained to the police. 11 Go away. 12 It is sunny. 13 I forgot him. (about him.) 14 English newspapers are sold here.

Exercise 26: 1 Lembro-me dele. 2 Não me sentia bem. 3 Queixámo-nos da comida. 4 Tem chovido muito este ano. 5 Já tinha posto a carta no correio. 6 Bebe-se muito vinho em Portugal mas os portugueses nunca se embriagam. 7 A janela estava aberta. 8 A lotaria foi ganha por uma mulher pobre. 9 A minha saia estava rota. 10 Foram todos presos. 11 Eles olharam-se um ao outro. 12 Não tenho viajado este ano. 13 Ouve-se muita musica inglesa em Portugal. 14 Não me quero servir. 15 Vimo-nos por acaso. 16 Aqui vendem-se jornais.

LESSON 9

Exercise 27: 1 It is necessary for them to study hard. (They must study hard.) 2 It is hoped they do not come in late. 3 Perhaps (Maybe) I will go out tomorrow. 4 I want you to do that at once. 5 Tell him not to come in until I call him. 6 I hope your wife is better. 7 I don't think he is a good football player. 8 We want a man who has the courage of his convictions. 9 Whether I like it or not I have to attend the meeting tomorrow. 10 Diga-lhe que não vá à reunião. 11 Embora eu não fale portûges muito bem, compreendo tudo. 12 Quer que lhe traga a lista dos vinhos? 13 É melhor que eu vá agora. 14 Não creio que haja jornais hoje. 15 Eles têm pena (Lamentam) que não possa vir esta noite. 16 Por favor não faça nenhum barulho.

Exercise 28: 1 It was a pity (a shame) he could not come. 2 I wanted you (*pl*) to learn Portuguese as quickly as possible. 3 I did not see any house that pleased me. (. . . that I liked.) 4 Perhaps he had already left. 5 If it were not so expensive, we would buy a farm in the Algarve. 6 We did not want you (*pl*) to bring presents. 7 I don't know whether it is raining. 8 If it rains I shall take an umbrella. 9 Until the factory workers go back to (resume) work, we cannot increase production. 10 Come to our house whenever you want. 11 As soon as you get a job in Mozambique, let me

150

know (tell me). 12 Do what you can. 13 Invite (*pl*) whom you wish.
14 He who (Whoever) wants to come along with me, let him come.
Exercise 29: 1 Assim que puderes, telefona-me por favor. 2 Se ele não
fosse tão preguiçoso (mandrião), não teria perdido esse emprego. 3 Foi
preciso que eles chamassem a polícia (*also:* Foi preciso chamarem a
polícia.) Disse-lhes para se irem embora. (*also:* Disse-lhes que se fossem
embora.) 5 Diga o que disser, eu não acredito que ela seja desonesta.
6 Quando me reformar escreverei muitos livros. 7 Faça como quiser.
(*also:* Faça o que quiser.) 8 Aconteça o que acontecer, e apesar do tempo
(clima) sempre amarei a Inglaterra. 9 Não havia ninguém que falasse
inglês. 10 Enquanto estiverem em minha casa, são meus convidados.
11 Lamentei que não pudessem vir. (*also:* Lamentei não poderem vir.)
12 Se você perdeu esta oportunidade foi porque quis. 13 Embora
protestassem (*or:* Tivessem protestado) a situação continuou a ser a
mesma.

*Note: The alternatives given above demonstrate the use of the personal
infinitive explained in lesson 10.*

LESSON 10

Exercise 30: 1 This book is for us to read. 2 I don't want to buy the car
unless you agree (without your agreeing). 3 It is a shame (a pity) you
cannot come next Sunday. 4 It was good (a good thing) that you brought
your coats, because it is going to be cold. 5 I fear they are cross with
me. 6 They did not come because they were tired. 7 It was impossible for
us to go to the bullfight. 8 You, winning the world cup? (*doubt and mild
derision implied*) 9 Eles vão partir antes de chegarmos. 10 Foi impossível
vermos o ministro. 11 Surpreende-me tu dizeres uma coisa dessas. (*also:*
Surpreende-me que tu digas uma . . .) 12 Disse-lhes adeus antes de
partirem. (*also:* . . . antes de eles partirem.) 13 Não posso dar uma
opinião até sabermos tudo. (*also:* . . .até que saibamos tudo. *or:* enquanto
não soubermos tudo.) 14 Não tivemos almoço (Não almoçámos) por não
termos tempo. (*also:* . . . porque não tivemos tempo.)

Exercise 31: 1 I have no time to write letters. 2 He went to Brazil for four
months. 3 My sister is going into hospital on Tuesday for an operation on
her throat. 4 I am telling you this for your own good. 5 I haven't hurt you
on purpose. (It was inadvertently that I hurt you.) 6 Last month I went to
Paris to visit my aunt. 7 Thank you for your kindness. 8 If it is left to me,
(Myself/As far as I am concerned/Personally,) I don't mind. 9 Não tenho
nenhumas notícias (novidades) para ti. 10 Ele lutou pelos direitos do
Homem. 11 Ele foi a Londres em negócios. 12 O senhor vai para casa
agora? 13 Por mim, o dinheiro seria abolido. 14 Peço desculpa
(Desculpe-me) por chegar atrasada/o. 15 Vou para a cama.

Mini-dictionary

Although the following is not an exhaustive list of words found in the book, it will be helpful as a quick reference. Numbers against some entries indicate pages where irregular verbs and other important words are explained. See pages 40–43 for days of the week, numerals and so forth.

a, an um, uma
able capaz; **to be able** poder
abolish abolir
abroad estrangeiro, no estrangeiro
accident acidente
address morada, endereço, direcção; **to address** (someone) dirigir-se a
admire admirar
advertise pôr um anúncio
advertisement anúncio
after depois de
afternoon tarde
against contra
agree concordar, estar de acordo
all todo/a/s
alone só, sozinho
allow permitir, deixar
almost quáse
already já
also também
always sempre
among entre
and e
angry zangado/a; **to be angry/cross** zangar-se com
animal animal
announce anunciar
announcement anúncio
any nenhum/a/s, qualquer, quaisquer
anybody ninguém, qualquer pessoa
anything nada, qualquer coisa
appear aparecer
apple maçã
arrival chegada
arrive chegar

as como, tão
as much/as many tanto/a/s
as soon as assim que
as soon as possible tão depressa quanto possível
ask (to enquire) perguntar
ask for pedir
at *page 24*
at least pelo menos
at once já, imediatamente
attend assistir a
aunt tia
awful terrível, péssimo

bad mau, má
badly mal
bank banco
banker banqueiro
bankruptcy falência; **to go bankrupt** falir
bath banho
bathtub banheira
bathroom casa/sala/quarto de banho, banheiro (*Br*)
be ser, estar *page 20*
beach praia
bear urso
bear (*v*) aguentar, suportar
beautiful lindo/linda, belo/bela
bed cama, leito
bedroom quarto (de dormir)
beer cerveja
before antes de, perante
begin começar, principiar
behind atrás de
believe crer em, acreditar em
beside ao lado de

besides além de
better melhor
between entre
big grande
bill conta
birthday aniversário; **to have a**
  birthday fazer anos
black preto, negro
blue azul
boat barco
book livro
book (*v*) marcar, reservar
boring/bored aborrecido *page 21*
both ambos
bottle garrafa
box caixa, caixote
boy rapaz
bread pão *page 50*
break (*v*) quebrar, partir
breakdown (car) avaria; **nervous b.**
  esgotamento nervoso
breakfast pequeno-almoço, café da
  manhã (*Br*)
bring trazer *page 140*
brother irmão
brother-in-law cunhado
brown castanho, marron (*Br*)
brush (*n*) escova, pincel
bull touro, toiro
bullfight tourada
bus autocarro, onibus (*Br*),
  machibomba (*Mozambique*)
business negócio, negócios
but mas
buy comprar
by por, através *page 24*

call (*v*) chamar; **to be called**
  chamar-se
can (= to be able) poder
car carro, automóvel
care cuidado; **careless** descuidado
carry levar
cat gato/a
certainly certamente, claro, com
  certeza

chance oportunidade; **by chance**
  por acaso
change mudança; (*v*) mudar, trocar
cheap barato
cheat (*v*) enganar, fazer batota
cheese queijo
chicken galinha, frango
child/children criança/crianças
choice escolha
choose escolher
Christmas Natal
church igreja
cigarettes cigarros
cigars charutos
citizen cidadão *page 50*
city cidade
clerk empregado
climb (*v*) subir
coach camioneta, carruagem
coat casaco, paletó (*Br*)
coffee café
cold frio
come vir; **come in** entrar; **come**
  back voltar
computer computador
complain queixar-se
complaint queixa
contents conteúdo
continue continuar
cost custo; (*v*) custar
count (*v*) contar
country país; **countryside** campo
course curso; **of course** com certeza
cousin primo/a
courage coragem
cover (*v*) cobrir
cross cruz; (*v*) atravessar; **to be**
  cross estar zangado, zangar-se
cup chávena, xícara
customer freguês, cliente
customs costumes, alfândega
customs officer funcionário da
  alfândega

daughter filha
day dia

dead morto
dentist dentista
die morrer
diet dieta
difficult difícil
dinner jantar; **to dine** jantar
dirty sujo
disappear desaparecer
dishonest desonesto/a
disappointed desanimado,
    desiludido, desapontado
do (v) fazer
doctor doutor, médico
door porta
dream sonho; (v) sonhar
dress vestido; **to get dressed**
    vestir-se
drink bebida; (v) beber
drive conduzir, guiar
drunk bêbado, embriagado; **to get
    drunk** embriagar-se
dye (v) tingír

each cada; **each one** cada cual; **each
    other** um ao outro
ear orelha, ouvido
early cedo
easy fácil; **easily** facilmente
eat comer
either ou
employment emprego
English inglês
enjoy divertir-se, gozar
enough bastante
enter entrar
equally igualmente
evening tarde, noite, tardinha
every cada
everyday todos os dias
everybody toda a gente, todo o
    mundo (Br)
everything tudo
except excepto
exam exame
examine examinar
example exemplo

exercise exercício
exhibition exposiçâo
expect esperar, contar com
expenses despesas
explain explicar
eye olho

fall (v) cair
far longe, distante
farm quinta
fast depressa, adiantado
father pai
fault culpa
favour favor
fear medo; (v) ter medo, temer,
    recear
feel (v) sentir, sentir-se
fetch buscar, ir buscar
few alguns, poucos
fight (v) lutar
fill encher
find achar
finish (v) acabar, terminar
fire fogo, incêndio, lume
flat raso; (apartment) andar
flight voo
floor châo, soalho, andar
flower flor
fog nevoeiro
follow seguir
foot pé; **football** futebol
for para *page 24/105*
foreign estrangeiro
forget esquecer, esquecer-se de
fork garfo
fortnight quinzena, quinze dias
fortunately felizmente
freeze gelar, congelar
French francês
friend amigo/a
from de *page 24*
fruit fruta
full cheio, pleno
furniture mobília; **pieces of
    furniture** móveis

garden jardim
general geral; (army) general
gentleman cavalheiro, senhor
German alemão *page 50*
get obter, arranjar
get up levantar-se
girl rapariga, moça
give dar
glass vidro, copo taça
go ir, ir-se embora
go out sair
gold ouro/oiro
good bom/boa; **goodness** bondade
good-bye adeus
goods mercadoria, géneros
grapes uvas
great grande
green verde
grow crescer
guess (*v*) advinhar
guests convidados

hair cabelo
half metade, meio
hand mâo *page 50*
happen acontecer
happy feliz
hardly mal
hat chapéu
have ter *pages 14/16*
hazard azar
head cabeça
health saúde; **healthy** saudável
hear ouvir
heavy pesado
height altura
help ajuda, socorro; (*v*) ajudar;
  help yourself sirva-se
here aqui, cá
high alto
holidays férias
home casa, lar
hope esperança; (*v*) esperar
horse cavalo
hot quente, calor
hotel hotel

hour hora
house casa
how como *page 31*
however contudo
hunger fome
hurry pressa
hurt (*v*) magoar, ferir
husband marido, esposo

if se
ill doente
immediately imediatamente
important importante
impossible impossível
in em *page 24*
increase aumento; (*v*) aumentar
information informação
intend tencionar
introduce apresentar
invite convidar
Italian italiano

Japan Japão; **Japanese** japonês
job emprego, trabalho
journey viagem
juice sumo, suco (*Br*)

keep (*v*) guardar, manter
key chave
kind amável; **kindness** amabilidade
king rei; **kingdom** reinado
knife faca
know conhecer, saber
knowledge sabedoria,
  conhecimento

lady senhora
lamp candieiro, lâmpada
large grande
last último
late tarde, atrasado
laugh (*v*) rir; **laughter** riso
law lei, Direito
lawyer advogado
lazy mandrião, preguicoso
learn aprender

leave (v) partir, sair; (let go) deixar
lemon limão
lend emprestar
less menos
lesson lição
let (v) alugar; (allow) deixar
letter carta
lie mentira; **to tell a lie** mentir
lie down deitar-se
lift elevador; (v) levantar, elevar;
  (in car, n) boleia, carona (Br)
light luz; (v) acender; (colour)
  claro
like como, semelhante; (v) gostar
Lisbon Lisboa
listen ouvir, escutar
little pequeno, pouco
live (v) viver
London Londres
long longo, comprido
long for (v) ter saudades de
longing saudade/s
look (v) olhar; **look for** procurar,
  buscar (Br)
lose perder
loud alto
love (v) amar, gostar de
low baixo
luck sorte
lunch almoço
luggage malas, bagagem
lukewarm morno

magazine revista
mail correio; (v) pôr no correio
majority maioria, maioridade
make (v) fazer; **made** feito
man homem
mankind homem, os homens, o ser
  humano, humanidade
manager gerente
many muitos
market mercado, praça
married casado; **to get married**
  casar-se
me/mine *page 57*

meat carne
meet encontrar, encontrar-se com
meeting encontro, reunião
memories memórias, recordações
message recado, mensagem
milk leite
mind cérebro, mente; (v)
  importar-se *pages 126/127*
mistake erro; **to be mistaken** estar
  enganado *page 22*
money dinheiro
month mês
more mais
moreover além disso, tanto mais
  que
morning manhã
most mais, a maior parte de,
  máximo
mother mãe
mother-in-law sogra
move (v) mover, transportar,
  mexer-se, comover; **move house**
  mudar-se
much muito
music música
must dever
my *page 57*

name nome
near perto de
nearly quáse
necessary preciso, necessário
need (v) precisar de
neighbour vizinho
neither nem
nephew sobrinho
never nunca, jamais
new novo
news notícias, novidades
newspapers jornais
next próximo, a seguir
nice simpático
niece sobrinha
night noite
no, not não
nobody ninguém

noise barulho
nor nem
nothing nada
now agora
number número

obey obedecer
of de *page 24*
officer funcionário
often muitas vezes, frequentemente
on em *page 24*
once uma vez; at once já,
    imediatamente
only só, somente, apenas
open (*v*) abrir
operation operação
opinion opinião
opportunity oportunidade
or ou
orange laranja
order encomenda; (*v*)
    encomendar, mandar, mandar
    vir
other outro/a
ought dever
our, ours nosso *page 38*
out fora
owe dever

page página
painter pintor
paper papel
parcel embrulho, pacote
park parque
part parte
partner sócio, parceiro
pay (*v*) pagar
pear pera
peas ervilhas
pen caneta
pencil lápis
people gente, pessoas
pepper pimenta
perhaps talvez
permit autorização, licença
person pessoa

photograph fotografia
pick up (*v*) apanhar
picture quadro, gravura
pin alfinete
pipe cano, cachimbo
pity pena, lástima
plane avião
plate prato
play (*v*) brincar, jogar, tocar *page
    65*
pleasant agradável
please por favor, faz favor, faça o
    favor; (*v*) agradar
pleasure prazer, gosto
pocket algibeira, bolso
police polícia
poor pobre
Portuguese português
possible possível
post correio; postman carteiro
pound (money) libra
poverty pobreza
prefer preferir
present presente
prevent prevenir, evitar, impedir
price preço
print (*v*) imprimir
promise prometer
proof prova
protest (*v*) protestar
prove provar
pupil aluno, estudante
purchase compra, compras
put (*v*) pôr; put in meter

quarter quarto
queen rainha
question pergunta, questão
quickly depressa
quiet calado

race corrida
railways caminhos de ferro
rain chuva; (*v*) chover
rare raro; (steak) mal passado
raw cru, verde

read ler
ready pronto
receive receber
recommend recomendar
red encarnado
refuse (*v*) recusar, recusar-se
regards cumprimentos
remain ficar, continuar
remember lembrar-se de
repeat (*v*) repetir
reply resposta; (*v*) responder
resolve (*v*) resolver, decidir-se a
respect (*v*) respeitar
rest resto, descanso; (*v*) descansar
result resultado
resume recomeçar, retomar
return (*v*) voltar, regressar
retire reformar-se, afastar-se
rich rico; **richness** riqueza
right (-hand) direito; (correct)
    certo; **to be right** ter razão
ring (*v*) tocar, telefonar
river rio
room quarto, sala, casa
run (*v*) correr

sad triste
safe cofre; **to be safe** seguro, salvo,
    livre
salary ordenado, salário
salt sal
same mesmo
sample amostra
satisfy satisfazer
say dizer
scarcely apenas, mal
schedule (on) a tempo, à tabela
school escola
scruples escrúpulos
sea mar
season estação
secret segredo
secretary secretária
see ver
seem parecer
send mandar, enviar

serious sério, grave
servant criada, empregada
several vários
shame vergonha
sheet lençol
ship barco, navio
shoe sapato
shop loja
short curto; **in short** em suma;
    shortly em breve
shortage falta
show espectáculo; (*v*) mostrar
shut (*v*) fechar, encerrar
silly tonto, parvo
silver prata
sing cantar
sir senhor
sister irmã
sit down sentar-se
sitting-room sala de estar/de visitas
situation situação
skirt saia
sleep (*v*) dormir; **to be sleepy** ter
    sono
slow lento, devagar
slowly devagar, lentamente
small pequeno
smell cheiro, aroma
smile (*v*) sorrir
smoke (*v*) fumar
so assim, portanto, tão
some algum *page 70*
something alguma coisa
sometimes às vezes
son filho
soon em breve; **as soon as** assim
    que, logo que
sorry desculpe; **to be sorry** ter
    pena, pedir desculpa
Spain Espanha; **Spanish** espanhol
speak falar
spend gastar
spoon colher
stamp selo
start (*v*) começar, principiar
station estação

stay (v) ficar
still ainda
story história, conto
street rua
strength força
strike greve
strong forte
study (v) estudar
sugar açucar
suit fato, terno (Br)
suitcase mala
sun/sunshine sol
supply (v) fornecer
sure (to be) ter a certeza
swim (v) nadar
swimming-pool piscina

table mesa
take tomar, levar, tirar page 26
tall alto
tea chá
teach ensinar
teacher professor/a
tell dizer, contar
telephone telefone
telephone call telefonema, chamada
television televisão
than que, do que
thank (v) agradecer; thank you
  obrigado/a
that pages 32, 34
the page 13
theatre teatro
then então
there ali, acolá, lá, aí
there is/are há
therefore portanto
these, this, those page 34
thing coisa
think pensar, crer, achar
thirst sede
throat garganta
throw (v) atirar
thunder trovoada
thus assim
ticket bilhete

time tempo, horas, vez
tired cansado
to a, para page 24
today hoje page 42
too também
too much demasiado, demais
tool ferramenta
touch (v) tocar, apalpar, mexer em
town cidade
train comboio, trem (Br)
travel (v) viajar
traveller viajante
trip volta, giro, pequena excursão,
  viagem; (v) tropeçar
true verdade, verdadeiro
truth verdade
try tentar, provar, experimentar
turn (v) voltar, virar

ugly feio
umbrella guarda-chuva,
  sombrinha, pára-sol
uncle tio
understand perceber,
  compreender, entender
understanding compreensão,
  entendimento
underneath debaixo de, sob,
  debaixo
unfortunately infelizmente
until até
upstairs em cima, lá em cima
useful útil

very muito
village aldeia, povoação
visit visita; (v) visitar
visa visto
voyage viagem

wait (v) esperar
waiting espera, à espera,
  esperando
waiter criado (de mesa)
walk (v) andar a pé, caminhar,
  passear

want (v) querer, desejar
warm quente, calor
wash (v) lavar, (oneself) lavar-se
watch relógio; (v) vigiar
water água
way caminho
we/us etc *pages 21/57*
weak fraco
weather tempo
week semana
well bem
what/when/where/which *page 31*
whether se
white branco; **whitewash** cal
who/whose/whom *page 31*
whole todo, inteiro
why porque, porquê
wife esposa, mulher
win (v) ganhar
wind vento; **windy** ventoso
window janela
wine vinho
winter inverno
wish desejo; (v) desejar
with com
without sem

woman mulher
word palavra
work trabalho; (v) trabalhar
workman operário, trabalhador
world mundo
worried preocupado, apoquentado, inquietado, aflito
worry (v) preocupar-se, apoquentar-se
worse pior
worth valor; **to be worth** ter o valor de, ser digno de *page 127*
wound ferida; (v) ferir
write escrever
writer escritor/a
written escrito

year ano
yearly anual, por ano, anualmente
yellow amarelo
yes sim
yesterday ontem *page 42*
yet ainda, no entanto, contudo
you/yours etc *pages 17/38*
young jovem
youth juventude

Index

The numbers refer to section headings, *not* pages.